· A HISTORY LOVER'S ·
GUIDE TO

LAWRENCE
KANSAS

• A HISTORY LOVER'S •
GUIDE TO
LAWRENCE
KANSAS

TRISTAN SMITH

WITH THE WATKINS COMMUNITY MUSEUM

THE
History
PRESS

Published by The History Press
An imprint of Arcadia Publishing
Charleston, SC
www.historypress.com

Front cover images: Statue of the 1941 "Fighting Jayhawk" by Dr. Eugene "Yogi" Williams. *Author's collection*; display of Polar Bears inside the Panorama exhibit in KU's Natural History Museum. *Author's collection*; the Robert J. Dole Institute of Politics. *Author's collection*; downtown's Granada Theater. *Author's collection*. *Back cover image*: Neon sign on the Lawrence Amtrak Depot. *Author's collection*.

First published 2025

Manufactured in the United States

ISBN 9781467158435

Library of Congress Control Number: 2024950522

Notice: The information in this book is true and complete to the best of our knowledge. It is offered without guarantee on the part of the author or The History Press. The author and The History Press disclaim all liability in connection with the use of this book.

For all my friends and family in Lawrence and Kansas City.

I miss you all!

CONTENTS

ACKNOWLEDGEMENTS

I know. What is a guy living in Houston, Texas, doing writing a book about the historic spots in Lawrence, Kansas? I grew up near Lawrence in Kansas City, Missouri. Much of my childhood was filled with stories of outlaws and renegades. I lived less than thirty minutes from where Jesse and Frank James were born and grew up, where the James Gang robbed some of their first banks and trains. In all that, I learned that some of those men who lived their lives on the run from the law got their start as guerrillas during the Civil War with William Quantrill. Men like Quantrill, George Todd, Frank James, Bloody Bill Anderson and Cole Younger—among so many others—attacked the city of Lawrence on the morning of August 21, 1863, killing hundreds and burning much of the business district and so many homes. *That* was my introduction to Lawrence.

As a kid, my family would take a day some weekends and shop down on Mass Street and see some of the historic sites before heading back home to Kansas City. As I grew up, I learned more about Lawrence—a deeper history, one that fleshed out the city, making its history so much more attractive to me. I learned about Langston Hughes, Bleeding Kansas, the University of Kansas, Haskell and more. I wanted to live there and be a part of that community. When I was an adult, I met a girl who grew up in Lawrence. We eventually got married (hey, Tanetti), had a couple of kids (hi, Theo and Max) and lived in Lawrence for about a decade before moving to Houston.

While we lived there, though, I tried to immerse myself into as much of the local history and community as possible. Our kids attended Lawrence

Community Nursery School (the Little Red Schoolhouse) for a bit, I worked at the University of Kansas's Natural History Museum and I served on the board of the Douglas County Historical Society at the Watkins Community Museum. Through many of the early museums I worked for, in Lawrence and in Kansas City, I was able to get involved in the formation of Freedom's Frontier National Heritage Area. These varied roles then led to a role as a historian for the City of Lawrence's Historic Resources Commission. I had never been more involved in the history of a city than I was in Lawrence. Over the years, I collected books, magazines, pamphlets and more relating to the history of Lawrence and its environs. With all this combined, this book is my sort of love letter to the city of Lawrence.

I would first like to thank Watkins Community Museum's executive director, Steve Nowak, and his staff (John Jewell, Will Haynes, Shannon Hodges, Sarah Lindsey, Kate Grasse, Andrew Stockman, Kennedy Murphy and Kacie Herbek) for their assistance and for keeping the history of Lawrence alive and relevant. I would like to thank Chad Rhoad, my acquisitions editor at The History Press, who has provided guidance, assistance and prodding to get this book to shelves. I would like to thank everyone in my past in Lawrence; there are too many to list them all, but Erin, David, Michael, Greg, Bruce, Theresa, Jen, Thomas, Bobby, Synthia, Kelly, Dawn, Ranjit, Teresa, Dale, Ann, Jerree, David, John, Judy, Steve, Lou and Emily, Tracey, Lindsay and Andrea (and I know I am missing so many others), you connected me with the community and the history of Lawrence in ways that made me feel a strong part of Lawrence.

Finally, I would like to clue you into a few resources I've found to be fruitful in writing this book and in my love for this great town. Of course, the *Lawrence Journal-World* newspaper (with many great articles and columns by Chad Lawhorn) and the *Lawrence Times* online newspaper (especially with the articles by realtor Tom Harper) are great resources for history and the day-to-day goings-on of Lawrence. For homes and architectural history of Lawrence's mid-century modern era, check out lawrencemodern.com. The city's Historic Resources Commission's documents and city registers have been invaluable (thank you, Lynne Braddock Zollner), as have the resources of the Lawrence Preservation Alliance; the histories collected by the University of Kansas, Haskell University and Lawrence's Visitor's Bureau (aka "Unmistakably Lawrence"); and the numerous organizations and community members creating such an amazing sense of place in Lawrence. Thank you!

Finally, to Sara, thank you for your continued support, love and encouragement in my writing career. I could not have done this without your belief in me and my writing. Thanks for putting up with me and cheering me on all while going on adventures and explorations with me. I love you.

A SHORT HISTORY OF LAWRENCE, KANSAS

Originally, the area now known as Lawrence was settled by the Kaw, or Kansa, people in the seventeenth and early eighteenth centuries. Following a series of treaties with the United States, the Kaws relinquished their land to the Shawnees, established in 1830; they too would eventually be displaced to make room for new settlers upon the opening of the Kansas Territory.

Following the passage of the Kansas-Nebraska Act in May 1854, the Kansas Territory was opened for settlement. The act, introduced by Democratic Senator Stephen A. Douglas of Illinois and signed into law by President Franklin Pierce, allowed for popular sovereignty to decide the slavery status of the new incoming state. If the people voted it as one or the other, that's what status the new state would have—repealing the Missouri Compromise and producing an uprising known as Bleeding Kansas, as both proslavery and antislavery activists flooded into the territory to make their decision known, as forcefully as possible, if need be, to sway the vote. While it was officially closed to settlement until 1854, the area already had squatter settlements, primarily north of the Kansas River, but it was also well known because the Oregon and California Trails ran parallel to the river and along Hogback Ridge, now known as Mount Oread.

Founded primarily for political reasons, the town of Lawrence was established by the New England Emigrant Aid Society. There was fear

Looking down from Mount Oread toward town, this view of Lawrence was taken by Robert Benecke in 1873, a time when Lawrence was experiencing a period of regrowth. *Courtesy of the DeGolyer Library, Southern Methodist University.*

throughout the North upon the passage of the Kansas-Nebraska Act that it was a surefire way to bring Kansas into the Union as a slave state, already sharing a border with the slave state of Missouri. Instead, it united antislavery forces into a movement to stop the expansion of slavery, creating the Republican Party as a political force to do so. Four men, in early May, traveled to the new territory to scout out new town locations: Thomas and Oliver Barber, Samuel Walker and Thomas Pearson. They settled on the land at the foot of Hogback Ridge and along the Kansas River and Oregon and California Trails.

Representative Eli Thayer of the U.S. House, Republican abolitionist and businessman Amos A. Lawrence and others began working to send new settlers to the area, known as Free Staters. Charles Robinson and Charles Branscomb would explore the territory and the townsite the scouts had selected, eventually settling on this location for their Free State town. The first pioneers set out for Kansas on July 17, 1854, arriving a few weeks later. At noon on August 1, they ate their first meal on Hogback Ridge, eventually renamed Mount Oread after the Oread Institute in Worcester,

Massachusetts. Multiple other parties and individuals followed. The new settlers began establishing their town, then called Wakarusa prior to settling on Lawrence, after the town's benefactor, Amos Lawrence. New laws and a government were established that were antislavery-friendly despite much surrounding opposition from proslavery settlers in the nearby area.

The city was platted out, featuring many of the same streets as you find today, with Massachusetts Street, better known locally as Mass Street, serving as the main north–south thoroughfare, named as such to commemorate the New England Emigrant Aid Company's home states. To the east of Mass Street, the north–south streets were named for the original thirteen colonies, with only Mass and New Hampshire Streets out of order (primarily because of the desire to have Mass Street serving as the primary street). Those streets west of Mass Street were named for states in order of admittance to the Union; however, sometime along the way, several streets were placed in the wrong order, and other states' names were never used. The state street naming process went away when Iowa Street was established, running through the center of Lawrence. The east–west streets were named after men who had done something in history in the "sacred cause of liberty." In 1913, the east–west streets were renamed to numbered streets.

The era of Bleeding Kansas had begun, and the town of Lawrence began growing exponentially; it was quickly becoming the face of the struggle over slavery, as well as the country's future. Conflicts raged throughout the east border of Kansas it shared with Missouri. Elections became farcical and, oftentimes, bloody, rarely leading to anything resembling forward motion.

This Alexander Gardner photo from 1869 shows Mass Street in 1867, just four years following Quantrill's Raid. *Courtesy of the Boston Public Library.*

Secret societies, known as Blue Lodges, began popping up. Weapons were being sent west by supporters for protection and war. Henry Ward Beecher was known to send arms in boxes marked "Bibles" in the hopes they would escape detection. Horace Greeley even sent a howitzer to town.

As the year 1855 dragged on, it became evident that bubbling tensions were about to boil over into armed combat. On August 27, 1855, an event occurred that might have broken the camel's back. Acting Territorial Governor Daniel Woodson appointed Samuel J. Jones to the office of Douglas County sheriff. Jones was an avowed supporter of slavery and didn't even live in Kansas, instead living in the proslavery hotbed of Westport, Missouri. Then, in October, following letters from his sons who had moved to Kansas earlier, John Brown arrived with a wagonload of weapons to fight off the proslavery settlers.

On November 21, 1855, proslavery settler Franklin Coleman shot neighboring Free State settler Charles Dow in the head, killing him after a land dispute. When Sheriff Jones investigated, he sided with Coleman over his self-defense stance and chose to arrest Dow's friend Jacob Branson for disturbing the peace. While Branson was quickly rescued, it tipped the balance, and the town of Lawrence began preparing for a fight. Jones mustered a small army of nearly 1,500 proslavery men and marched on Lawrence. Charles Robinson was chosen to direct the defense, with James Lane selected as second in command with a committee of safety to help keep watch. John Brown arrived with his four sons, and five earthwork forts were constructed. On December 8, Governor Shannon managed to broker a peace treaty, begrudgingly, to the Wakarusa War.

The following spring, on April 23, 1856, Sheriff Jones entered Lawrence to arrest about a dozen members of the extralegal Free State legislature, a rogue government in opposition to the proslavery territorial government. In the ensuing commotion, Jones was shot and injured by Charles Leonhart and was driven out of town. They offered a bounty for the sniper's arrest, disavowing the act, but it didn't help. This time, Federal Marshal Israel B. Donaldson, Sheriff Jones and Missouri Senator David Rice Atchison raised another army, marching on Lawrence to destroy the symbol of the antislavery movement, the Free State Hotel. On May 21, Charles Robinson's home was seized for their headquarters and later burned (Robinson had been arrested earlier and was in prison near Lecompton for treason); the offices of the antislavery newspapers were attacked, with type smashed and tossed into the river; and the Free State Hotel was shot with a cannon and burned down.

Taken by Amon Gilbert DaLee, this photo depicts a seated Dr. John Doy among his rescue party, known as "The Immortal Ten," during the summer of 1859. They had freed Dr. Doy from a Missouri jail, where he was being held for allegedly abducting slaves. *Courtesy of Kansas State Historical Society.*

Additional battles, murders and conflicts waged throughout the region over the next few years, but the conflict began to slide more toward political activity. The Lecompton Constitution failed to make Kansas a slave state, and the county seat was moved from Lecompton to Lawrence. By the election of 1857, Free Staters had gained the upper hand and ousted the proslavery majority from the legislature. Samuel Jones resigned his post and left the territory in early 1858, and the antislavery legislature began meeting often in Lawrence, thus functioning as the de facto capital of the territory from 1858 until statehood in 1861, while Lecompton was still the de jure seat. On October 4, 1859, the Wyandotte Constitution was approved, and Kansas was admitted as a Free State following approval by Congress, on January 29, 1861. This admission immediately followed the departure of the seceding states' proslavery congressman and led the country into civil war.

Throughout the war, Lawrence remained a stronghold for the antislavery movement. Guerrilla units, known as Jayhawkers or Red Legs, called Lawrence home, led by the likes of James Lane, James Montgomery, Charles "Doc" Jennison and others. They would cross the

Taken by Alexander Gardner on his 1867 continental trip, this image was taken from former Civil War entrenchments atop Mount Oread, looking toward downtown Lawrence.

state line, raiding western Missouri, stealing goods, freeing slaves and burning down farms. On August 21, 1863, in retaliation for this and many other instances—both perceived and real—William Quantrill led hundreds of his guerrilla followers into Kansas on another raid, this time targeting Lawrence. Most of the houses and businesses here were burned, and roughly two hundred men and boys were murdered. Lawrence somehow managed to rebound and did so in a spectacular fashion. Following a bitter winter, rebuilding continued into 1864. This time, the citizens organized themselves into protective companies, and the federal government erected several military posts, such as Camps Ewing and Lookout and Forts Ulysses and Union, atop Mount Oread. No further attacks were made on Lawrence during the war.

Part of the reconstruction and revitalization included a new university. Attempts were made to construct a university in 1855 but only moved forward once Kansas garnered statehood. The debate, from 1861 to 1863, was where it would be located—Lawrence, Manhattan or Emporia. When Manhattan was made the site of the state's land grant college on January 13, 1863, it left Lawrence and Emporia. Lawrence won by one vote, and in 1866, the University of Kansas opened. Following the establishment of KU, the United States Indian Industrial Training School, a Native American boarding school with the goal of assimilation, was opened in 1884. The school continues to be in operation and has expanded beyond its original purpose to become one of the leading Native American universities in the country—now known as Haskell Indian Nations University, named for Dudley Haskell, the legislator largely responsible for the school being in Lawrence.

The first railroad to connect Lawrence from Kansas City was built in 1864, and the first train to cross the Kansas River in Lawrence followed in November 1867. This would lead to exponential growth along the river and throughout Lawrence. A dam over the river was completed and opened for good in 1879 by James Gower and his son-in-law, Justin DeWitt Bowersock. A wind-powered mill was constructed in 1863 and continued to operate until it was destroyed by fire in 1905.

The early twentieth century saw an upsurge in popularity and prosperity in Lawrence. Watkins National Bank opened in 1888 and lasted until 1929. Jabez B. Watkins's widow, a philanthropist, donated the building to the city for use as a city hall. It operated as such until a new city hall was constructed in 1970, after which the bank was converted to reopen as the Watkins Community Museum. Multiple other banks would open along Massachusetts Street, better known as Mass Street, and new businesses, industry, restaurants, entertainment venues and retail operations would lead to a thriving downtown district. Streetcars would give way to a bus system, and Woodland Park, an amusement park on the city's east side, would last from 1909 to the 1920s. Lawrence Memorial Hospital opened in 1921, expanding from fifty beds to a large complex today. In 1929, a small municipal airport opened on the north side of North Lawrence.

Given the downturn in the local economy, the downtown district began declining with it. In the 1970s and 1980s, the city and district saw a resurgence of popularity. Clinton Lake opened southwest of the city, adding another form of entertainment. In November 1983, however, Lawrence became a hotbed of national discussion following the airing of the television movie *The Day After*. First shown on ABC, it was later shown in movie theaters around the world. It depicted what would happen if the United States were destroyed in a nuclear war. The movie was filmed primarily in Lawrence, and hundreds of residents appear in both speaking roles and extras. Additionally, the Eldridge House, the keystone of downtown Lawrence's historic district, was reconverted from apartments back into a hotel during this period.

Today, Lawrence's downtown is a hotbed of activity and the center of Google's universe. Concerts, festivals and numerous events take place here, drawing both residents and visitors to the numerous restaurants and shops. Lawrence's Meadowbrook Apartment complex is the default starting point for Google Earth, set by former complex resident Brian McClendon, a 1986 KU grad and director of engineering for Google Earth. Historic preservation downtown and throughout the city is a primary focus, as many residents pride themselves on their historic properties. From a city that counted just more than 1,500 residents in 1860, it has grown to a city of more than 100,000 residents, surging well over that during the school year with the students on campus.

EAST LAWRENCE AND THE WAREHOUSE ARTS DISTRICT

Roughly bounded by Massachusetts and Delaware Streets on the east and west and 6th and 11th Streets on the north and south, the East Lawrence neighborhood was originally a disputed area claimed by both the Emigrant Aid Company and Missourian/proslavery advocate John Baldwin, who arrived in the area first. The dispute was finally settled in 1855 when the Emigrant Aid Company recognized Baldwin's right to his land. In response, early emigrants viewed East Lawrence as being dominated by proslavery squatters.

Eventually, the neighborhood became an area of great diversity, with Americans, Germans, Irish, French Canadians and formerly enslaved people and free Blacks settling here. Following the Civil War, the neighborhood became a more ethnic, working-class neighborhood. Housing here was cheap and was located near where most of the emigrants were working, businesses downtown, industrial areas by the river and the rail lines. The neighborhood was filled with boardinghouses, restaurants, mills, breweries, foundries, meatpackers and manufacturers in an area now transformed as the Warehouse Arts District. Closer to the river, the neighborhood featured the Bottoms, Lawrence's red-light district. The Bottoms contained many illegal and illicit businesses and sported gin and juke joints lining New Jersey, Pennsylvania and Delaware Streets between 9th and 7th Streets.

Built in 1947, Municipal Stadium was dedicated during a Lawrence Colts semiprofessional baseball game before a crowd of 2,500 fans. The stadium, now adorned with the Dave Lowenstein–led mural project "The East Lawrence Waltz," which depicts the neighborhood's history, continues to be used today. *Author's collection.*

ABE & JAKE'S LANDING

8 East 6th Street

Abe & Jake's Landing, a local landmark as an event and bar venue, originally was constructed in 1893 for the Consolidated Barbed Wire Company. When it was operating at peak production, the building was filled with more than three hundred workers, making it the largest employer in Kansas at the time.

Albert Henley—later a state representative, senator and Lawrence mayor—founded the Lawrence Barbed Wire manufacturing company, a predecessor to the Consolidated Barb Wire Company, the building for which still stands. He had previously manufactured barbed wire on a smaller scale prior to moving from Iowa to Kansas in 1878. By 1883, his Lawrence operation had merged with several other smaller companies to create Consolidated Barbed Wire. The building you see now was erected in 1891. Just outside the factory, fishermen could make a full-time living off the river's supply of catfish. The nearby grain elevator would spill out and slip into the waters below, not only attracting the fish but also helping them grow to a large size. Two fishermen who had a fishing cabin next to the barbed wire company facility were Abe Burns and Jake Washington, namesakes of today's event venue.

The building has gone through a variety of uses since the barbed wire business was sold in 1899. In 1907, the Lawrence Paper Company purchased the building, using the facility until 1974. Once the paper company moved out, the building became semi-abandoned, sported a leaky roof and featured zero windows but has since been restored.

A.J. AND MARY CARROL GRIFFIN HOUSE

645 Connecticut Street

When Civil War veteran Andrew Jackson "A.J." Griffin and his wife, Mary, arrived here in 1867, they found Lawrence in rapid expansion, both in population and in the postwar economy. In Lawrence, they transported groceries to southern Kansas for a local wholesale grocery store while also delivering stone for the construction of the new Southern Kansas Railroad.

A.J. established a thriving business of lime, sand and stone and secured the contract for helping construct the Bowersock Dam in 1877, eventually becoming the city's primary stone supplier. In 1882, he added to this a retail coal and wood yard and, in 1891, a lucrative ice business. Mary became a major leader in the town's women's suffrage movement and a champion for education and diversity. By 1901, the new couple from Illinois had become one of the wealthiest and most recognizable couples in town. As a result, they had this home built, and it reflects that upward movement.

The Griffins hired Alexander Shaw, who had served with A.J. on the city council and in numerous projects, to build their dream home. The result was this Queen Anne–style home featuring numerous state-of-the-art advances, including steam heating, electric lighting and plumbing. This new house also allowed Mary to host lavish parties, a reputation she had gained, and for them to be featured along with the home in the media. Located in the East Lawrence neighborhood, the home is clearly an anomaly from its neighbors, as it stands out from the homes that are more for working- and lower-middle-class families.

SANTA FE DEPOT

409 East 7th Street

When the Santa Fe Depot opened its Lawrence Station in East Lawrence in 1956, it replaced a previous depot that had been built on the same lot in 1883 but had been extensively damaged during the 1951 flood. Demolition of the damaged building began in April 1955, with the completion of this iteration coming in February 1956.

While most cities were planning on jettisoning their city stations, Santa Fe saw a good investment in services for Lawrence—combining the massive influx of student enrollment with those world war veterans continued well into the 1950s. When passenger rail service was taken over by Amtrak in 1971, this station continued to serve passengers as an unstaffed Amtrak station for passengers on their single route connecting Los Angeles to Chicago.

The depot has achieved numerous ups and downs since its 1950s construction but has always served as a nostalgic landmark in town. A $1.5 million project in 2011 provided the public with an accessibility platform and much nicer lighting and signage. In 2017, Burlington Northern Santa Fe Railway donated the historic building to Lawrence, which was followed up with more renovations.

The Santa Fe Depot in East Lawrence continues to operate to this day and is a popular destination for those traveling between Los Angeles and Chicago on Amtrak. Its blue neon sign and architecture have made it a local favorite and led to its restoration in 2017. *Author's collection.*

JAMES AND MARY REED HOME

731 New York Street

When Mary Langston died in March 1915, the future poet Langston Hughes moved in with family friends James and Mary Reed at 731 New York Street. With the Reeds, he attended services and Sunday school at the New York AME Church and classes at New York Elementary School, both nearby. He left Lawrence later in the year to join his mother in Illinois. He first published in *The Crisis*, not long after, in 1921, his signature poem "The Negro Speaks of Rivers." Eventually he became one of the biggest names in the Harlem Renaissance. His autobiography, *The Big Sea*, was published in 1940.

THEO POEHLER MERCANTILE

619 East 8th Street

Located in what is now called the Lawrence Warehouse Arts District, the Poehler Building was constructed in 1904 and used as a wholesale grocers' storage for Theo Poehler Mercantile Company. This four-story grocer distribution warehouse is adjacent to the railroad tracks in East Lawrence. German immigrant Theodore Poehler built the warehouse to support his grocery business, which he established in 1889 with his brother August. Later

Located in what was once a bustling warehouse district in East Lawrence, the Poehler Loft Apartments were constructed in 1904. Originally, the building served as a wholesale grocer's storage for the Theo Poehler Mercantile Company. *Author's collection.*

branch houses were established at Emporia in 1900 and Topeka in 1917. Once part of a thriving industrial district, it stands as one of the area's only survivors. It has remained unchanged since that time, especially its exterior. After sitting vacant for many years, the building was purchased in 2001, with the hopes of converting it into usable living space. Today, the warehouse has been rehabbed into the Poehler Loft Apartments, which features forty-nine units in East Lawrence.

ST. LUKE'S AME CHURCH

900 New York Street

Organized in 1862, St. Luke's AME Church services were originally held inside of a blacksmith's shop in the 700 block of Massachusetts Street. The congregation began construction on a new church building, located at the corner of 9th and New Hampshire, in 1863 and were well underway when Quantrill's guerrillas struck town. That morning, a company of twenty-five military recruits was camping here. Twenty of the men were killed and tossed into the foundation trenches. Construction halted and was eventually abandoned following the raid. A stone building was erected at the rear of a lot at 900 New York Street, bordering the alley. Members of the congregation included escaped slaves, freed slaves and their families, many of whom had come to Lawrence through the Underground Railroad. This newer Gothic Revival building, built in 1910, replaced the earlier iteration; future poet Langston Hughes and the Reed family, with whom he lived, were frequent attendees of services and Sunday school here. He would later recount seeing vaudeville entertainer and fellow Lawrencian Nash Walker (of the famed Williams and Walker act) perform at the church.

TURNHALLE

900 Rhode Island Street

Having previously met in Miller's Hall downtown, Lawrence's Turnverein constructed Turnhalle in 1869, serving as the center of German American

Once a beehive of activity within Lawrence's German community, Turnhalle operated from 1869 until anti-German sentiments during World War I caused a dramatic drop in attendance and altered the focus of the building and its organization as the American Gymnastic Union. *Author's collection.*

life in town until the outbreak of World War I. German immigrants would gather here for community events, to socialize in their beer garden and to use the building's fitness center. Many who frequented the building lived nearby, along the western edge of East Lawrence. It is the oldest standing building on the western edge of East Lawrence. Turnhalle was a great place of activity and remains as one of the few surviving Turnvereins in the United States. In the hall itself, there was an emphasis on gymnastics training and competition, but also for meeting, celebrations, music, theatrical performances and holiday parties.

Anti-German sentiments following the onset of World War I eventually led to the closure of the hall and changed the society's name to the American Gymnastic Union. Rod Ernst, who would later become the operator of downtown's Ernst Hardware and whose family had been members of Turnverein, sold the stone building to Lawrence Preservation Alliance in 2012. LPA identified the repairs needed to stabilize the building, received a protective easement and had it listed as a landmark in the Lawrence Register of Historic Places to ensure that it would always be preserved.

NEW YORK SCHOOL

936 New York Street

New York School, established in 1869, was one of the first schools to open in Lawrence. From fourth through sixth grade, future poet Langston Hughes attended New York School. When his grandmother died, he lived with family friends at 731 New York Street, just a few doors down the street. His book *Not Without Laughter* is a fictionalized account of his childhood in Lawrence. The original school building was erected on this exact site but no longer stands, as it was torn down to make space for the newer school you see today.

This modern iteration was constructed in 1937 as part of President Franklin D. Roosevelt's New Deal public works program. Making up the north end of the main hallway, four classrooms were added in 1955. Another addition, renovation work, was completed in May 1996, including a new gymnasium with a kitchen and the conversion of the old gym into a media center with a mezzanine computer lab. To commemorate the old school building, stonemason and stone carver Karl Ramberg, father of former New York School alumnus and artist Zoey Ramberg, created a stone tablet, placing it near the southwest corner of the present school building. In 2022, the school board approved a public Montessori program for New York School, adding that approach to its pre-K and K–5 classrooms.

REUBEN LUDLINGTON HOUSE

938 Rhode Island Street

Reuben Ludlington arrived in Lawrence in 1857, relocating from Springfield, Massachusetts. He constructed this National Folk House–style home in 1859 and lived here from 1860 to 1863. During Quantrill's Raid, Ludlington operated a cigar and tobacco shop on Mass Street. While the store was ransacked, both the store and his home survived. Luckily, Ludlington did too, as he was back east on a buying trip. During the raid, then Mayor George Collamore perished in the melee. When Ludlington returned from his buying trip, he became Lawrence's mayor and oversaw the rebuilding of the town; he earned reelection terms in 1876 and 1878.

He also sold his home on Rhode Island Street in 1863 to John Stillman Brown, a Unitarian minister. Brown had also moved to Lawrence in 1857. He was elected the superintendent of school for Douglas County twice, also serving stints as city clerk and on the state board of agriculture. The modest one-and-a-half-story, ell-shaped brick home features an arched window in the peak of the façade gable. Brown had previously been a member of the Horace Greeley "Brook Farm" community and founded the *Kansas Farmer* publication. His son, William, moved to Kansas, settling in Emporia in 1862, and was admitted to the bar in 1864, becoming the judge of the Ninth Judicial District of Kansas in 1867–77 and was a member of the 44th Congress from 1875 to 1877.

HENDRY HOUSE

941 Rhode Island Street

Reverend William Aiken Starrett was serving as a military chaplain at Fort Leavenworth, twenty-five miles north of Lawrence, before a small military detachment traveled to Lawrence in mid-August 1863 with its chaplain, Reverend Starrett. He secured lodging at 941 Rhode Island with the owners of the home, Judge James M. Hendry and his wife, Rebecca. Somehow, this house, and the reverend, were spared the wrath of Quantrill's Raid. His exact whereabouts during the raid are still unknown, but his influence and support following in the days after were greatly needed. Sixteen days following the raid, the elders of the Presbyterian church in Lawrence officially asked Starrett to remain as a pastor in their community. He accepted and participated in the rebuilding of Lawrence and helped bury the loved ones lost. The home is a Kansas Landmark. Once Starrett was officially in his position, he rented four rooms in one of the largest homes downtown and traveled to Ohio to get his future bride, whom he married in Xenia in February 1864 before returning to his new home of Lawrence.

SHALOR ELDRIDGE HOME

945 Rhode Island Street

This National Folk–style brick home was once the most valuable single property on the city's east side. Constructed in 1857, the Shalor Eldrige family lived here while Lawrence was being constructed. Consisting of two rectangular brick sections, the two-story home received a later frame addition to form an ell to the north and features a one-room brick outbuilding located behind the home. Rather plain in its exterior appearance, it does sport a front and south side porch.

Shalor Eldridge arrived in the territory in 1855 and immediately got involved in the Free State movement. Previously, he had worked in the railroad industry in the Northeast before moving west. When he arrived in Kansas City, he bought the American House from Samuel Pomeroy. The hotel building would eventually become a rendezvous point for many Free State men and a place of refuge for the proslavery Governor Andrew Reeder upon his escape from Kansas Territory under duress in 1856.

Eldridge moved to Lawrence with his family around the same time, leasing the Free State Hotel at Lawrence and then building this home in 1857. During his life, he would establish a daily stage line that crossed the Missouri-Kansas border at multiple points in 1857, was appointed a paymaster in the Union army in 1863 and after the Civil War served as a Douglas County commissioner, was elected city marshal of Lawrence and built a number of other hotels in Kansas City, Missouri; Coffeyville, Kansas; and Atchison, Kansas. When he arrived in the territory, he quickly earned the reputation of one of the leading entrepreneurs in Kansas. However, by 1874, he was facing financial ruin as he suffered through a national depression. He remained in Lawrence until his death in 1899 and is buried at Oak Hill Cemetery. His home remains a residential property. In 1979, the home was substantially rehabilitated, with the owners reusing existing material; they were also able to retain important historical features of the house.

HOBBS PARK

702 East 11th Street

Speer moved to Lawrence with his wife and eight children in 1855. He went on to publish one of the first Kansas newspapers, the antislavery *Kansas Pioneer*, a predecessor to the current *Lawrence Journal-World*. He would continue to promote the antislavery movement and African American civil rights throughout his life, as well as playing a vital role in the founding of KU and Baker University. However, during Quantrill's Raid, Speer lost two of his sons (John and Robert), managing to escape death himself by hiding in a corn field. Afterward, he helped put out fires, delivered a detailed report to Topeka and rebuilt his home at 909 Pennsylvania Street. That home is in Hobbs Park, located about three hundred yards northeast of its original location.

Speer finished the home between 1866 and 1869, and it was saved from demolition in 2000. Hobbs Park was created to serve as a beacon of hope and as a symbol of perseverance in the fight against injustice. The park contains a basketball court, a baseball field and playgrounds. On the back of the stadium, a mural is dedicated to the history of Lawrence and includes the city's Native American history, poet Langston Hughes, Quantrill's Raid and John Speer.

Located in Hobbs Park, this small home belonged to John Speer and his family. Speer published the antislavery *Kansas Pioneer* newspaper and actively promoted civil rights. While he escaped the 1863 raid, two of his sons were not so lucky. *Author's collection.*

SAMUEL A. AND KATE RIGGS HOUSE

649 East 11th Street

Built by politician and governmental lawyer Samuel A. Riggs, this home was constructed from 1863 to 1864. Riggs and his wife, Kate, moved to Lawrence in 1859, with Samuel becoming the region's district attorney his first year in town. It was still being constructed at the time of Quantrill's Raid and suffered extensive damage but stood as one of the few to survive the raid. When the raiders arrived, Riggs narrowly escaped with the help of his wife. He escaped death by taking shelter in his old home on Rhode Island Street. When a raider called for him to come out, he did. As the raider aimed to shoot, Kate grabbed the horse's bridle, causing it to bolt, and a clean shot could not be fired. The horse

Samuel and Kate Riggs's home was still under construction when Quantrill's raiders hit town in 1863. The home suffered extensive damage, some of which can still be seen on its brick walls, when raiders attempted to burn the home. Both Kate and Samuel survived the carnage that day. *Author's collection.*

dragged Kate around, and when they finally settled, the raider aimed at Samuel once again. Kate interfered again by grabbing the reins, allowing Samuel to escape successfully.

The construction crew had, by that time, built the walls and frameworks for the doors and windows, but the fire burned all the wood. The Riggs family restarted construction immediately and moved into the home in November 1864. Samuel and Kate lived in the home until 1914 before moving to be closer to their son in Ann Arbor Michigan. They would rent out the home until they sold it in 1931. It continues to be used as a private residence, and it is said that burn marks from the raid are still visible on the brick walls of the home.

LA YARDA

8th and New Jersey Streets

La Yarda was Lawrence's vibrant Mexican American community, located in East Lawrence. Located in this area was a housing complex for railway workers and their families that was constructed in the 1920s. At the time, rail companies relied heavily on Mexican immigrants and migrant workers, many of whom came to the states seasonally to work before returning home to their families in Mexico. The construction of the housing complex was used to entice the migrant workers to stay in town so they could continue to work on the railroads.

The complex consisted of several housing units that surrounded a courtyard, with a pump that supplied water to the residents of La Yarda. Within the complex, a strong community built up and expanded with a common play area, community picnic spaces and shared produce and livestock. Unfortunately, it was a time of extreme prejudice. Part of the reason to band together was due to the fact that many of the residents felt a sense of separation from the rest of Lawrence; many spoke Spanish instead of English at home, their children's names were Anglicized at school and segregation was still rampant throughout town, including at the public pool and the movie theaters.

In 1951, Lawrence was affected by a massive flood. The Kansas River overflowed its banks, rising through the streets and sweeping through La Yarda. It came so quickly that residents had only enough time to grab essentials before fleeing the complex. Once the waters subsided, they found the area unsalvageable. The water, in some places, had risen to the roof, leaving behind in its wake water damage and piles of mud. Only some of the remaining concrete foundations of La Yarda exist, found with a short hike into the nearby woods. The rest of the complex was destroyed by either the flood or its aftermath.

HENRY WATERS HOUSE

1125 New Jersey Street

When Henry Waters and his wife, Helen, along with their family, arrived in Lawrence during the late 1860s, the city was in a building boom. Henry established a branch of his uncle's C. Wakefield & Company patent medicine business. The company was part of a vast patent medicine trade, much of which was fortified with ingredients such as morphine, cocaine or opium among the simple herbs or vegetables and alcohol. Henry was just one of several thousand agents, all claiming that nearly every illness, pain or injury could be cured with their medicines.

In 1872, Waters had this Italianate two-story home constructed for his family. The home demonstrated the popularity of patent medicines at the time, with the newspaper calling it the "finest residence in southeast Lawrence." The home's cellar, with entrances inside and out, was used by Waters to produce and distribute the patent medicines. During the Panic of 1873, the Waterses were hit hard economically and moved to a farm near Iola, Kansas, where Henry began working at a mill and raising stock.

WOODLAND PARK SITE

East 12th Street and Prairie Avenue

Owned by the Lawrence Light & Railway Company and later operated by the Lawrence Amusement Company, Woodland Park was an amusement park located on the east side of town. It opened in 1909 where Brook Creek Park exists today. The park covered forty-three acres of woods between the

The Daisy Dozer, located in East Lawrence's Woodland Park, is seen here circa 1915. It was one of the United States' earliest roller coasters when it opened in 1910. *Courtesy of the Watkins Community Museum.*

northernmost residences of Brook Creek neighborhood, the Public Works Yard and the Burlington Northern Santa Fe Railroad tracks. One popular feature of the trolley park was Daisy Dozer (aka Casey's Coaster), a wooden sit-down roller coaster. In addition to the roller coaster, there was a merry-go-round, a shoot-the-chutes, a dance hall, a Ferris wheel and a bandstand. Its location near the railroad allowed the park to draw in traveling carnivals and circuses. Later, the park added a half-mile horse racing track, a football field, a dance pavilion and a baseball diamond.

After the park closed in the early 1920s, many of the buildings and rides were left abandoned. For the next few decades, the park sat unused and fell into disrepair. The land was offered to the city for free if the land were to remain a park. Instead, the city wanted the land for industrial usage, and the offer was rescinded. After a stalemate, the city finally purchased the land and promised that the "Nature Woods Area" would remain an undeveloped wooded nature preserve. When the 1951 flood swept along the Kansas River, much of what was left of the old park was washed away. You might still be able to find a foundation for one of the rides, possibly the Daisy Dozer, but most of where that once existed is now heavily overgrown.

OAK HILL CEMETERY

1605 Oak Hill Avenue

Lawrence's mayor in 1864 urged the city to build a new cemetery, as most raid victims were buried at Pioneer Cemetery. Its location in town made it difficult for people to visit and to maintain. It was considered forgotten, and graves were often left unmarked. The city purchased land for a new cemetery, and it was first constructed in 1866 as a means for the people of Lawrence to memorialize those killed in Quantrill's Raid. Designed in the rural cemetery design, it featured rolling hills, curving paths and numerous trees, becoming more a parklike setting than an open cemetery. Several prominent Kansans are buried here, including former Governor Charles Robinson, Senator James Lane, Lucy Hobbs Taylor, John P. Usher and Langston Hughes's grandparents Charles and Mary. For years, there were Decoration Day observances at Oak Hill to commemorate Quantrill's Raid.

Located at Oak Hill Cemetery, this monument was dedicated in 1895 in honor of the memory of those residents killed during Quantrill's Raid. Commemorative events for those who lost their lives in the massacre, and reunions for those who survived, began in 1891. *Author's collection.*

By 1895, enough funds had been raised to erect the large monument located near the center of the cemetery to honor those victims. The city continued to improve the cemetery throughout the late 1890s, including the installation of a sidewalk running to and from downtown.

Located atop a central hill inside Oak Hill Cemetery is the Quantrill's Raid Memorial. Dedicated on May 20, 1895, it was placed here in the memory of the nearly two hundred residents killed on August 21, 1863. Commemorations to those who lost their lives in the massacre began on August 21, 1891, organized by the Association of Survivors of Quantrill's Massacre. This citizens' monument to the victims was unveiled in 1895, with an inscription reading: "Dedicated to the memory of the one hundred and fifty citizens who defenseless fell victims to the in-human ferocity of border guerillas led by the infamous Quantrill in his raid on Lawrence, August 21, 1863."

LIBERTY MEMORIAL CENTRAL MIDDLE SCHOOL

1400 Massachusetts Street

For several years, Lawrence's Old High School, which had been built in 1889 at 9th and Kentucky, was exceeding its capacity—at one time nearly three times its maximum occupancy. Needing a larger school, the school board decided to build a monument to address this need. The city constructed Liberty Memorial High School here in 1923, with a dedication ceremony taking place on August 27, the fifth anniversary of the American defense in the Argonne. Serving also as a memorial to honor Lawrence residents who died in World War I, the school recognizes the roughly 300 young people from Lawrence who fought in the Great War. Of those who fought, 144 had yet to graduate high school; 19 of them were killed either in France or at home or overseas due to disease; and 6 high school girls became nurses, with 2 of them perishing during the war.

The exterior of the Liberty Memorial features several symbolic figures. Most notably are those of men in military garb to represent the soldiers lost in the war and shocks of grain, located in the keystone of the middle archway, that represents Kansas, the Wheat State. The school's auditorium can seat 1,500 and was the largest in the state when it opened. The building also features eighteen stained-glass windows from Belgium, donated by one of the early 1930s classes. They represent the regiments of the honored men.

In 1930, the lion was chosen to serve as the school's symbol. In 1946, Chesty Lion became the high school's official mascot. Until this time, out behind the main school, there was an old church that the school used as a study hall and print shop. There, journalism students produced *The Budget*, the school's bimonthly newspaper. Today, a tennis court sits in its spot. In 1954, Lawrence High School moved to Louisiana Street for more space and modern accommodations, and the Junior High School moved into this building.

BARKER NEIGHBORHOOD

Located adjacent to the East Lawrence neighborhood to the south is the Barker Addition, running from 11th Street to 23rd Street on the north and south and from Massachusetts to the Burroughs Creek Rail Trail on the west and east, respectively. Originally, this was prairie land located to the south and east of the original Lawrence townsite. Farms and homes began to dot the area shortly after the settlement of town. Named after George Barker, two-time mayor, one of the main features running through the Barker neighborhood is the Burroughs Creek Rail Trail. Other streets in the neighborhood are named for numerous early settlers, such as the families of Lathrop and Susan Bullene, Oliver and Anna Hanscomb, Oscar and Mary Sophia Eldridge Learnard and former Mayor Barker (1887 and 1907). The Bullene family moved to Lawrence in 1857, remaining here for the rest of their lives. During this time, Lathrop built a successful mercantile business in Kansas City and Lawrence, the latter of which was the precursor to downtown's Weaver's Department Store. The Hanscombs put down roots in Lawrence in 1854, while Oscar Learnard was a leading local lawyer and newspaper editor married to Shalor Eldridge's daughter, Mary Sophia.

Covering more than 2.9 acres, today's Sunrise Project was once a popular garden center operating from the 1920s through 2013. *Courtesy of the Lawrence Preservation Alliance.*

DR. JAMES NAISMITH MEMORIAL-MEMORIAL PARK CEMETERY

1517 East 15th Street

Located in Memorial Park Cemetery, this large memorial commemorates the life of Dr. James Naismith, inventor of the game of basketball. Naismith was born on November 6, 1861, in Ontario, Canada. Thirty years later, he was working as a physical education teacher at the International YMCA Training School in Springfield, Massachusetts. He was charged with the task of developing an indoor game that could capture the interest of students confined inside during cold weather, and he had fourteen days to do it. By taking and adapting elements from other games, Naismith developed thirteen basic rules guiding play on a court that featured a peach basket at each side of the court as goals.

In 1898, Naismith was hired by the University of Kansas to develop its physical education program and coach a newly formed basketball team.

This statue of basketball inventor Dr. James Naismith is located at Memorial Park Cemetery. The monument honors not only Naismith, who is buried here, but also the lineage of coaches through the Kansas Jayhawks basketball teams. *Author's collection.*

Naismith coached the Jayhawks until 1907, ultimately ending his KU coaching career with a losing record but remaining on in the department as athletic director. The first games he managed had to take place off-campus in a local skating rink because KU's facilities were completely inadequate. By the turn of the century, enough colleges had basketball teams that intercollegiate play was finally possible. Naismith retired from his position at the university in 1937.

Naismith was struck with a fatal brain aneurysm at his Lawrence home in 1939. He is buried at the memorial with his wife and is surrounded by plaques of other KU coaches. He is also honored by the Naismith Memorial Basketball Hall of Fame in Springfield, Massachusetts. Additionally, his original rules are on display within the Allen Fieldhouse complex.

KIBBEE FARMSTEAD

1500 Haskell Avenue

Walter and Fannie Kibbee built this two-story Dutch Colonial home in 1908. The Kibbees purchased the land from Mary Coffin, an elderly woman who had not been living on the land. They purchased the land in 1871 but lived in Iowa; as such, no improvements were made during that time. Eventually, they built the home, along with the farmstead that featured a few outbuildings that are still extant, including a barn, shed, chicken house, outhouse and garage. The gravel drive leads from both Haskell Avenue and East 15th Street, passing the outbuildings. The couple raised cattle, milk cows, poultry and swine, along with three acres of alfalfa.

The Kibbees sold the farm to C.D. Stewart in 1919, moving to San Diego. Stewart turned around and sold the property the following year, and then the Altenbernds bought the farm in 1924, owning it until 1972. Eventually, what once was a farm on the outskirts of the city became annexed in 1959. The new owners, the Wamsleys, began to sell off portions of the farm, including a lot to the International Order of the Odd Fellows (IOOF), with the remaining five acres being purchased by David Frayer in 1989. The home has only been slightly modified since construction and is listed in the National Register of Historic Places. It was an unusual farm for the region, remaining a small-scale subsistence farm while many others transitioned to large cash crop operations.

THE SUNRISE PROJECT

1501 Learnard Avenue

Covering more than 2.9 acres across the northern edge of the Barker neighborhood, 1501 Learnard Avenue was the longtime site of a popular garden center. Constructed in the 1920s, the garden center operated until the end of 2013, when the last owner put it up for sale. David and Susan Millstein purchased the property, intending to keep the historic 1920s buildings and accompanying greenhouses and utilize the space to promote community, gardening and social justice through an organization called the Sunrise Project. This organization continues here hosting events, workshops and plant sales along with maintaining a community orchard.

WILLIAM BURROUGHS HOUSE

1927 Learnard Avenue

Beat writer, artist and counterculture leader William S. Burroughs moved to Lawrence in 1981. He lived here longer than anywhere else in his life. After meeting and befriending Lawrence resident James Grauerholz in New York City, the two became lovers. Grauerholz would later serve as Burroughs's agent and editor, luring him away from New York to Lawrence in the hopes of a more stable life. Burroughs arrived in Lawrence in 1981, briefly moving into a stone house a few miles out of town before purchasing this home, a two-bedroom red and white bungalow. Here, he lived with his three cats, maintained a small garden, shot his guns and could often be seen walking to Dillon's, the neighborhood grocery store. He was active in Lawrence's underground art scene, and his fame followed him. Guests here included Kurt Cobain, Timothy Leary, Patti Smith, Michael Stipe, Allen Ginsberg, Steve Buscemi, John Waters, Norman Mailer and others. He also continued to write and create works of art.

Burroughs died in 1997, with a wake being held at Liberty Hall. His estate owns a private home and has not opened it to the public. His belongings are located away from the home in secure storage, and the house is used primarily to host meetings or the occasional private guest of William Burroughs Communications, headed up by Grauerholz. The home was added to the Lawrence Register of Historic Places in 2005, and the nearby creek received a federal designation in 2004, being renamed Burroughs Creek.

ROBERT MILLER HOME

1111 East 19th Street

The Miller family lived in South Carolina when Kansas Territory opened to settlement. They belonged to an antislavery church and had heard of the abolitionist movement in the new town of Lawrence. Patriarch Robert moved to Lawrence in 1854, building this home before bringing the rest of the family to the territory in 1858. Son Josiah founded the *Kansas Free State* newspaper, and Robert was a farmer and salesman. While not very political, Robert did host public legislative meetings in a room above his store.

The property surrounding the home, the smokehouse specifically, became a stop on the Underground Railroad. In 1863, when Quantrill came around,

Robert Miller's property once served as a stop on the Underground Railroad. Nearby, on the morning of August 21, 1863, Quantrill's raiders stopped and killed Reverend Samuel S. Snyder while he milked his cows; he was the first victim of the raid. *Author's collection.*

the raiders stopped not far from the Miller House and killed Reverend Samuel S. Snyder, minister of the United Brethren Church and chaplain to Black Union troops. Snyder was in his cow yard, located along the road, milking his cows. The group halted as soon as they were within range and commenced firing. Reverend Snyder fell immediately, the first victim of the raid. The home is one of the very few remaining, and well-maintained, houses in Kansas from the territorial period. Its appearance has changed very little.

AFRICAN AMERICAN QUILT MUSEUM AND TEXTILE ACADEMY

2001 Haskell Avenue, Suite 206

Located in the studio of acclaimed textile artist Marla A. Jackson, this home doubles as a museum for the artist's narrative quilts, which are inspired by the oral histories of her ancestors and the region. Born in Michigan among a family of artists, she moved to Kansas at the age of eighteen. She now teaches textile arts to local youth, and besides narrative storytelling through quilting, she offers classes in batik, fabric dyeing and fabric painting.

Ms. Jackson's quilts have been displayed in the American Folk Art Museum, the Smithsonian's Museum of African American History & Culture and the Smithsonian's Anacostia Community Museum, as well as dozens more throughout the country. Two quilts on display here of note are said to have been made by Maria Rogers Martin, an African American woman among the enslaved people who were stolen from the Wayside Rest Plantation and led to Kansas on foot by Union troops in the winter of 1862. She would become a paid servant of Colonel Charles "Doc" Jennison, leader of Jennison's Jayhawkers during the Civil War. The studio is open only by appointment for tours of the studio and teaching gallery and is part of the National Underground Railroad Network to Freedom.

ROANOKE

2235 East Drive

Roanoke is a Queen Anne cottage built in 1894 for Martha Gillette Babcock, widow of Carmi Babcock, who served as Lawrence's first postmaster general and its second mayor. Babcock's Addition started in 1858 when he purchased a large section of land south of 14th Street, located mostly at East and West Drive, between Vermont and Tennessee. Carmi married Martha in 1866, and this home was built to replace a previous home consumed by a fire. The only homes in the addition still standing that are older than Roanoke are the two stone buildings to its west. Located at 2239 West Drive, they are the barn and carriage house, plus a worker's home, which remain from a previous home on the property. Multiple owners have lived in the house over the years, including one family who resided here for nearly thirty years. That family installed candle-powered carriage lights, rejiggered to be electric now, from an Iowa barn for use on the porch. In addition to the porch, another outstanding feature is the cupola on the upper level of the home.

OLD WEST LAWRENCE

The neighborhood of Old West Lawrence, known affectionately as OWL, got its start in 1855. It is roughly bordered by 6ᵗʰ and 9ᵗʰ Streets to the north and south, Missouri Street to the west and Arkansas Street to the east. Shortly after the settlement of town, new residents began branching farther east and west, away from downtown, and drew in wealthier and more socially and politically prominent residents. The area was a target of Quantrill's raiders when they attacked in 1863, and only five homes, constructed in 1860 and 1861, that survived the raid are still standing. Old West Lawrence was the first national historic district designated in Kansas, featuring 126 historic homes. Many have changed very little in their outward experience since their construction.

THE MARTIN HOUSE

601 Louisiana Street

Constructed in 1914, this house is an outstanding home running along 6ᵗʰ and Louisiana Streets. The front porch of this Neoclassical home of tan brick and native stone sports full-height Corinthian porch columns. The home was constructed for Theo Poehler Company executive Otto B. Guffler and his wife, Myrtle. While Guffler operated a major warehouse on the east side of town, he was likely not the most well-known resident to live here.

The widow Emily Hoyt operated a boardinghouse in this home during William Quantrill's Raid. She begged the raiders to spare her home—her only source of income—while her son hid behind the property. *Author's collection.*

For several years, the home belonged to KU Professor of Ecology and Evolutionary Biology Larry Martin and his wife, Jean. Martin was a famed vertebrate paleontologist and a curator at the National History Museum and Biodiversity Institute at KU. Throughout his career, he led field expeditions that collected more than 200,000 specimens and helped design twenty-two museum exhibits, including the Mosasaur hanging above the Natural History Museum entrance. His work with collections manager Desui Miao and preparator David Burnham on the flight properties of four-winged gliders and a possibly venomous dinosaur pushed their work to the forefront of paleontology.

The KU Natural History Museum's vertebrate paleontology collection and exhibits are immense, many originally designed by Larry Martin. That includes this Tylosaurus (a type of Mosasaur) that hangs inside and above the museum's main entrance. *Author's collection.*

The Martin home has since been rehabilitated by new owner Amy Lee, a KU law school graduate. She purchased the property in 2020, giving it extensive repairs and updating the mechanical fixtures to bring it to a more modern state of livability. Highlights of the project feature the home's restored third-floor great room and a refurbished grand entry hall leading to the staircase.

BUFORD M. WATSON PARK

Kentucky and 7th Streets

The location of Buford M. Watson Park was originally a wooded ravine when the first settlers arrived, separating downtown from West Lawrence. In the original plat of the city, the space was known as Central Park. A single bridge spanned the ravine when Quantrill's raiders hit town. The heavily wooded ravine served as a hiding place for many residents during the raid. While looking for victims on the other side of the ravine, the raiders rode across the bridge, killing several men in what is the present-day Old West Lawrence neighborhood. The corn fields and hilly terrain allowed others to escape unnoticed that morning.

The ravine has since been cleared and mostly filled in to serve the community as a park. Located here and nearby are a playground, the historic Santa Fe Steam Locomotive No. 1073 and the city's pool, the first integrated one in the city. This park is named for Buford M. Watson, who served as Lawrence city manager for nearly twenty years. He began in this position in 1970 and continued until his untimely death in October 1989. During his tenure, Watson's accomplishments included the beautification and revitalization of the downtown, public parks, recreation centers and more.

THE KILLING OF MAYOR COLLAMORE

646 Louisiana Street

George Collamore, an ardent Massachusetts abolitionist, moved to the newly opened Kansas Territory in 1856 with his family. When he arrived, he became an agent of the New England Kansas Relief Committee, providing food and supplies to other new territorial settlers. When the Civil War erupted, he was commissioned as a brigadier general and named the quartermaster of Kansas. Removed from the position in 1862, he was elected mayor of Lawrence. He took the reins in 1863 and was only in office a few months before William Quantrill's guerrillas attacked.

Awakened by shouts surrounding his house, he found himself surrounded, with no means of escape save a well outside. When the raiders entered the home, he managed to escape, lowering himself into the well, followed by a friend seeking a similar refuge. As his home burned to the ground, his eighteen-year-old son was severely wounded, but the rest of the family managed to escape. Collamore and his friend, however, succumbed to smoke inhalation. Just a few streets west along 7th Street, at Jerome Griswold's boardinghouse, a similar fate met four inhabitants. There, guerrillas shot Griswold; Josiah Trask, editor of the *Lawrence Journal*; Simeon M. Thorpe, a state senator; and Harlow Baker, a known Jayhawker. Baker was the only one of the men to survive their ordeal.

Once the raiders left, a close friend of the mayor's, Mr. Lowe, went down the well in hopes of rescuing him. The rope broke, sending Lowe to his death as well. Once the three bodies were removed, Collamore's body was returned to Boston for the funeral. Both he and his son were laid to rest at Auburn Cemetery in Cambridge. The location of the well is denoted by a marker laid nearby in the sidewalk.

LITTLE RED SCHOOLHOUSE

645 Alabama Street

Lawrence's "Little Red Schoolhouse," officially known as Lawrence Community Nursery School (LCNS), was founded in April 1948 by a coalition of parents. Located in Old West Lawrence, it was founded at a time when schools and other institutions were still segregated. The coalition of parents wanted to buck that trend.

Two major members of that coalition were Magdalene "Maggie" Carttar and Dr. Helen Gilles. Carttar was a major fixture in Lawrence's education opportunities for children, including Head Start, while Gilles graduated from KU Medical School and performed her pediatric internship and residency in Berkeley, California, before starting a practice in Lawrence and

Hundreds of Lawrence kids have attended the cooperative Little Red Schoolhouse in Old West Lawrence since its founding in 1948. Parents get involved not just as parents but also as leaders and supporters of the school. *Author's collection.*

at the Student Health Service of Haskell Indian Nations University, among serving with a variety of organizations throughout town. The coalition sought to provide cooperative, interracial and low-cost education.

As it was a cooperative, parents became involved, and their support and leadership in maintaining the school and building awareness became crucial. The school moved to its present location, into the building seen now, in 1957. LCNS continues to provide Lawrence families with a preschool education that is cooperative, interracial, low cost, diverse and inclusive by covering education through constructive and creative play while engaging children through language, art, sensory play, math and science.

THE MERC CO-OP

700 Maine Street

In 1933, Glenn Turner helped his parents open a grocery store in this location, eventually running Turner's Grocery with his wife, Rena. Turner's

Grocery would serve the Old West Lawrence neighborhood for more than four decades before closing in 1977 as one of the last family-run grocery stores in town. The family sold the property to the Community Mercantile, known today as the Merc Co-op.

Established in 1974, the Merc opened its first storefront in 1975 in downtown. Not long after, it moved its operations to the old Turner's Grocery building, transforming an old bait and tackle outbuilding into its bakery. Eventually, its popularity caused another move, this time in 1993 to 901 Mississippi. Originally a bowling alley and dance club called Palladium, it is now a Cork & Barrel Liquor Store, and it isn't hard to see the old bones of a grocery store here. It moved one final time, in 2001, to its current location at 901 Iowa Street, itself a former grocery store. The Turners' old grocery store building was purchased from the Merc by KU professor of architecture Dan Rockhill. Rockhill repurposed the building for residential use, resurfacing it with a stucco finish. The two-story home to the east once served as a parking lot for the two grocery stores.

WITTER S. MCCURDY HOUSE

909 West 6th Street

The Witter McCurdy House was constructed around 1869, during Lawrence's post-raid building boom of 1864–73. McCurdy was an active real estate developer who had moved to Lawrence from New York in 1858. He pounced on the boom by purchasing several properties in 1868, including the lot for this home. Built in the Folk House Federal style, which was popular among the New England immigrants, the three-acre homesite, when constructed, sat outside the city limits, so much so that a street didn't run in front of the house until the 1880s. Two years later, Witter sold the house to his brother Jesse, who moved into the home with his wife, Emily, and their four children. When Jesse and Emily died, the home was left to the children, with whom it stayed until 1917. They sold the home to African American musician Kathryn Leighton and her husband, John, who used the house primarily as a rental property and sold the home after World War II.

LANGSTON HUGHES HOMESITES

726, 732 and 736 Alabama Street

Looking at the home located at 732 Alabama, it may not look like much history occurred here, but this is the site of the poet Langston Hughes's grandmother's house, demolished in the 1960s. The home built here afterward has since been converted into a duplex. Langston lived here in Old West Lawrence with his grandmother from his birth in 1902 until her death in 1915. Langston's maternal grandparents Charles and Mary Langston had moved to Lawrence in 1886, where they raised their children and Langston. Charles Langston also owned acreage along the southern edge of the Kaw River oxbow, which dwindled to twenty-six acres following his death in 1892. His grandmother Mary Sampson Patterson Leary Langston was the widow of Lewis Sheridan Leary, one of the men killed during John Brown's raid at Harpers Ferry.

Poet Langston Hughes, seen here around 1925, was a Lawrence native, referencing the town numerous times in his works. His lineage follows back to Lewis Sheridan Leary, one of the men killed during John Brown's raid at Harpers Ferry. *Courtesy of the Schomburg Center for Research in Black Culture, New York Public Library.*

The neighboring brick home to the south, located at 736 Alabama, is probably a better indicator of what the home may have looked like during his childhood. While deeds to the entire east side of Alabama Street do not list Charles and Mary Langston as the owners, they did sell lots here around the turn of the century. It was here that they established homes for themselves and their son Desalines Langston. His home, located at 726 Alabama, still stands.

JOHN ROBERT GREENLEES HOUSE

714 Mississippi Street

Nestled in the Old West Lawrence neighborhood, this area was platted immediately following the Civil War. Future Senator James Lane purchased

120 acres of the tract. Known as Lane's First Addition, the land was situated between Tennessee and Mississippi Streets. Possibly constructed by James Lane, who lived up the street, for use as a parlor house, this two-and-a-half-story National Folk–style home was built over five phases, beginning in 1865. Charles A. Faris, who established the proslavery *Lecompton Union* and would later work for the *Lawrence Journal*, put a south addition on the house prior to 1870 and likely reoriented the east-facing house to face Mississippi Street instead. An 1873 west addition and new front transformed the home into a side-entry house. Additionally work came in 1911–12, including on the roof and porches. The back porch opens into the backyard, which features a garage that once served the house as a carriage house or barn.

When J.R. Greenlees moved into the home in 1893, and again in 1899, he made a major expansion of the house. Since 1911, the exterior of the home has changed very little, retaining much of its overall historic character since that time. Greenlees was a nationwide wholesale potato farmer and later the founder of the Mutual Oil Company and six other oil companies. He lived here from 1893 to until his death in 1947. Various families have lived in the home since.

EMILY HOYT'S BOARDINGHOUSE

743 Indiana Street

Emily Hoyt's boardinghouse continues to stand as one of the oldest buildings in Lawrence. Constructed by Hiram Towne, this home was one of the few that managed to survive Quantrill's Raid. As the raiders approached the west side of town, with very little notice of their arrival, Emily Hoyt's son hid behind the property to avoid detection. His mother, Emily, begged the raiders to spare her home when they arrived, claiming that she was a widow and that the home served as a boardinghouse, her only means of income. They spared her home and, in turn, her son's life.

FIRE STATION NO. 1

746 Kentucky Street

When the Lawrence Fire Department was organized in 1859, it did so as a volunteer organization called Republic Engine Company No. 1. The old engine room was inside a barn located at 11th and Vermont before it moved into the Market Building, later to serve as city hall, at 8th and Vermont Streets. This original Station No. 1 stood at that location for more than 140 years.

The force would continue to grow, adding a new station located at 19th and Massachusetts in 1928, but as methodology and equipment advanced, the old stations were too small. In 1949, the original Station No. 1 was torn down, and a new, more modern station, housing the fire and police departments, was built in its place. When the police department moved into its own facilities on 11th Street in 1976, the space was converted into the Douglas County Senior Resource Center.

In 1952, the fire department expanded service delivery by adding emergency medical response at the new station. In 1997, the department combined its emergency response force with the Douglas County Ambulance Service, which created the Lawrence-Douglas County Fire and Medical Department. This station was completely gutted in the late 2010s

Fire Station No. 1 replaced the original 140-year-old station in 1949. Built to house both the fire and police departments, it now houses the fire-medical services for the city and the county's senior resource center. *Author's collection.*

and completely renovated in a yearlong process. Covering seven stations and two support facilities in the region, the force responds to nearly twelve thousand calls annually and provides service to the city of Lawrence, KU and Haskell.

DUTCH WINDMILL

9th and Emery Streets

The landscape of Lawrence once had a large grinding windmill, located near here, on a high hill at the west end of Warren Street; it was a landmark for several years. Twelve Swedish immigrants arrived in Lawrence in 1863, brought in specifically to build the mill. When Quantrill's raiders arrived in August of that summer, the men were still working on the almost completed mill. They fled, managing to survive the onslaught. The raiders attempted to burn the windmill but only managed to burn some newly arrived lumber.

Standing atop a forty-foot foundation, the octagonal and cone-shaped mill stood five stories tall with a twenty-foot-diameter revolving dome and cap. In July 1885, it made its last run. It remained a landmark until it burned during the fall of 1905. No one was sure what started the fire, but it is suspected that it was set by parties smoking in the abandoned mill's basement. When

Lawrence's Old Dutch Windmill, seen here about 1903, stood for nearly four decades before burning to ruin in 1905. *Courtesy of the Library of Congress.*

the fire department arrived, the hose was not long enough to reach the fire from its closest hydrant. Two firefighters were sent back for a second hose cart, but this time, the pressure was not enough to extinguish the fire. The mill was completely consumed.

KLOCK'S WINDMILL GROCERY

900 Mississippi Street

Constructed from 1921 to 1922, Klock's Windmill Grocery building symbolizes an evolution of commerce for this part of town, from that of a grocery operated by European immigrants to businesses that now cater largely to students and the university. Fred Klock, a German American businessman, moved to Lawrence in 1880, settling in its expanding German community. He owned a grocery store as early as 1901 that had opened in the 1890s.

When Fred died in 1933, his son Helmer took over the business. He had been managing the store since 1925 and ran it until his death in 1940 at age forty-four, leaving the operation to his mother, Sophia, Fred's widow,

Today home to a restaurant and bar, this building originally served as home to two long-standing grocery stores and later the Independent Laundry and Dry Cleaning Company, the country's first automatic, coin-operated dry cleaning center. *Author's collection.*

who would manage it for two more years until she passed. R.M. Reeves purchased the building, operating it as Reeves Grocery until 1959, when he felt it was no longer viable to operate a neighborhood grocery.

Ed Elam, owner of the Independent Laundry and Dry Cleaning Company, leased the building, converting it to a 24/7 self-service laundromat; added a parking lot; and installed twenty automatic dry cleaning machines. It became the nation's first automatic, coin-operated dry cleaning center. While Elam died in 1963, the west portion of the building continued as a self-service laundry until 2018. Most recently, the location has served as home to a restaurant and bar.

ASAPH K. ALLEN HOUSE

945 Kentucky Street

Constructed in 1862, this two-story brick home managed to survive Quantrill's Raid. Located in what is today the Oread Historic District, it was designed by architect Ferdinand Fuller, a leader of the New England Emigrant Aid Society and member of the first party to Lawrence. Fuller built the National Folk–style brick nine-room house for Asaph King Allen, an early Free State settler in Lawrence in the 1850s. Allen was born in 1801 in New York and was buried at Oak Hill Cemetery following his death in May 1871. Fuller became Lawrence's leading architect in the city's early years, although many of his major works have since been razed or otherwise destroyed. Some of his other works include the original Free State Hotel (now the Eldridge) and KU's first building, the three-story Old North College. He passed away in 1886 and is also buried at Oak Hill Cemetery.

The house sat vacant and was in foreclosure for several years. During its 2020 rehabilitation project, the wood windows in the original portion of the house were restored and the exterior brick was repointed. The original front porch has been reconstructed, and the structure now serves as a duplex rental home, including the ability to rent it out through short-term accommodation apps.

NORTH LAWRENCE

The land north of the Kansas River originally contained the lands that were reserved for the Delaware tribe through a September 1829 treaty with the United States. On May 26, 1854, four days before President Franklin Pierce signed the Kansas-Nebraska Act into law, two Missourians, Clarke Stearns and John Baldwin, ventured over the Missouri border and staked out claims here. Baldwin operated a rope-drawn flatboat ferry from 1855 until the arrival of the Leavenworth, Lawrence & Galveston Railroad put it out of business.

Originally known as the town of Jefferson, it was renamed North Lawrence in 1869. The principal business streets in the area were Bridge and Locust Streets, and much of North Lawrence saw industrial growth as well. In 1870, following a previously failed attempt at annexation, the two cities finally consolidated. The area was also home to Bismarck Grove, a popular park that hosted fairs, picnics and temperance meetings until 1899. However, flooding was always a major concern. Minor floods in 1901 and 1902 were followed by a massive flood in 1903 and again in 1951. While Bowersock Dam helped to curb the issue somewhat, the damage caused by these two floods specifically saw the growth of North Lawrence slow to a snail's pace, but it is seeing a resurgence in popularity. The Lawrence River Trail today is located along the north bank of the Kansas River, running along the top of the flood-control levee. Following the nine-mile trail will afford you views of downtown Lawrence, as well as the nearby farmland

Construction on Lawrence's first railroad bridge to cross the Kansas River began in 1863 and was completed that December. It is seen here in an 1867 photograph taken by Alexander Gardner. *Courtesy of the Library of Congress.*

and the river. Keep an eye out in the winter for nesting bald eagles. The old retail stretch, serving as a pseudo-downtown for North Lawrence, contains a few well-established restaurants and a small handful of retail operations.

KANSAS RIVER BRIDGE

Highway 59, North of 6th Street

While the Kansas River, also known as the Kaw River, was once a meandering prairie river, the Army Corps of Engineers have channeled and tamed it. It is part of the extensive Mississippi River drainage system and part of the southwestern-most part of the Missouri River drainage system. Much of its watershed is dammed for flood control but is generally free flowing, with only minor obstructions. Its largest obstructions are the diversion weirs and the low-impact hydroelectric Bowersock Dam, located here at the river bridge off 6th and Massachusetts.

Bowersock Dam serves as the only hydroelectric power station in Kansas. In the early days of settlement, Lawrence pulled its energy from wood and imported fuel, but local timber resources were becoming depleted by the late 1860s, causing Lawrence to look at alternatives. Following structural issues and floods that impeded the construction of a stone dam, in 1878,

From this vantage point, one can see both the historic and new Bowersock Dam structures, as well as a downtown stretch of 6th Street, including the Consolidated Barbed Wire Company building, now home to Abe & Jake's Landing. *Author's collection.*

the property was purchased by James H. Gower, who passed it along to Justin De Witt Bowersock, his son-in-law. Bowersock continued to expand and improve the dam over the years, eventually allowing the city to pull electricity from its operations.

Despite a few instances, including a small break in 1885, the dam withstood floods under Bowersock. In 2011, BMPC broke ground on a new powerhouse on the north end of the dam, which significantly increased its power output when it was completed in 2013. Trails along the north side of the river, and vantage points from the south, allow great views of the Bowersock Dam.

THE LYNCHING OF PETE VINEGAR

6th Street and Kansas River Bridge

Located on the Kansas River Bridge is a marker telling the tragic story of the lynching of Pete Vinegar. Between 1865 and 1950, there were at least twenty-three documented racial lynchings in Kansas, three of those in Douglas County. Pete Vinegar's family was not an unknown entity to the Lawrence police. Money was always tight for Pete and Eliza, freed slaves from Arkansas, and their seven children. Due to their reputation, work was hard to come by, which caused their fourteen-year-old daughter, Margaret "Sis" Vinegar, to turn to prostitution.

On the evening of May 31, 1882, a meeting between Sis and David Bausman, a forty-two-year-old wealthy white man, became tragic. Sis's boyfriend, George Robertson, and Isaac "Ike" King decided to rob the man, boasting about it around town. When Sis and Bausman met that night, Bausman was assaulted but unexpectedly fought back. In the melee, Bausman was killed; his wallet was taken and his body tossed in the river before the trio returned to the Vinegar home. The police caught up with the trio and tossed Pete Vinegar in with the lot of them for good measure, despite no involvement. Reporters picked up information about an imminent lynching, but Sheriff Asher remained skeptical until one hundred disguised men gathered out in front of the jail. Using crowbars and sledgehammers, they broke into the jail, dragged the three men to the bridge and hanged them. No one ever stood trial for the lynching, and Sis was sentenced to life in prison for the murder. She died of tuberculosis in Lansing Prison, near Leavenworth, at the age of twenty-one. For decades, the men's bodies were buried in the northeast corner of Oak Hill Cemetery, a potter's field. In 2001, city employees found the men's names on a cemetery plot chart.

JOHNNY'S TAVERN

401 North 2nd Street

Johnny's Tavern has been serving customers since 1953. Originally this building was constructed in 1910. When it opened in North Lawrence, it operated with a grocery store on the main floor, with a hotel operating above the store. J.D. Bowersock, who owned the mill across the river, constructed this building. Following that, it served as a pool hall, another grocery store and finally a gin joint, operating until 1930. During the 1940s, the building was sold to Slim Wilson, who sold tractors and other farm implements. One of his side gigs in the building was offering gambling and serving cold beer.

In 1953, John Wilson, aka "Johnny," opened a new tavern here, calling it a "haven for the working man." It catered to those industrial workers who

Johnny's Tavern has been operating as a bar and restaurant since 1953, but the building originally served as a grocery store and hotel. Since that time, the restaurant became so popular that it expanded outside of Lawrence to surrounding cities. *Author's collection.*

worked and lived in the Lawrence area, especially those in North Lawrence, and in the industrial area of East Lawrence. The tavern sported a jukebox and cold beer, and it has been a local favorite for sports fans since. The original red arrow and giant beer mug that Johnny hung outside still hang out there today. In 1978, rugby players Rick Renfro and Doug Hassig took over the fledgling business by adding a grill and started serving burgers to their customers. In 1982, the duo brought in Louie Riederer, another fellow rugby player, who helped convert the upstairs hotel rooms into a private club, Up & Under. It was a private club until 1987, when Kansas adopted liquor by the drink. It exists to this day, although it has changed somewhat with the times.

Six years later, in 1993, during an expansion of the building toward the north, employees unearthed the gravestone of Betty Gailes, which had washed downriver during one of the numerous floods. They decided to name the new addition Betty's. The year 1991 saw the establishment get another expansion, this time out of North Lawrence and toward Kansas City and Johnson County, Kansas. It would later expand to Topeka, Kansas, and Parkville, Missouri. The restaurant now boasts thirteen locations in Kansas and Missouri.

UNION PACIFIC DEPOT

402 North 2nd Street

Charles Francis Adams, president of the Union Pacific Railroad, wanted to build a bigger, better depot for the burgeoning line running through town. Adams turned to Boston architect Henry Van Brunt, who had just established his office in Kansas City with partner Frank Howe. Adams had the original smaller and utilitarian depot demolished to make way for the new depot, which Van Brunt designed as a blend of French vernacular and Richardsonian Romanesque. It opened for service in 1889. The new station became a focal point for students coming from and going to the college town, as well as a point of departure and arrival for soldiers during both world wars. It also managed to survive two of the most devastating floods to hit Lawrence, in 1903 and 1951, when it filled with thirty inches of water.

Serving Lawrence for decades before closing in the 1970s, it stayed unused for several years prior to a 1991 restoration project. When the railroad finally discontinued its freight service in 1984, it announced plans to tear down the building within the week. The community rallied to save the building, resulting in the restoration project. The project included the restoration, repair and cleaning of the exterior, replacing the steeple that had been

Located north of the river, Lawrence's Union Pacific Depot opened for service in 1889 and closed in the 1970s. Following a restoration project in the 1990s, the building served as the city's Visitor Information Center. *Author's collection.*

removed in the 1920s, a new canopy and the reconfiguration of its interior. In 1996, the station reopened, this time as the city's Visitor Information Center. While the center has moved to a more prominent location downtown, the space continues to be used as a public meeting facility.

WILEY'S GROCERY

401 Elm Street

North Lawrence is separated from the rest of town by the Kansas River. Partly because of this, it retains a character all its own. The area sports a very small stretch of commercial buildings that served as a pseudo-downtown district for the neighborhood. One of the key commercial properties is located at 401 Elm Street. This stucco-clad two-story building features decorative window drip caps and masonry corbeling along the roofline. Constructed between 1869 and 1872 by James L. Canavan, it originally served as a broom factory. It was one open space on each of three levels, a basement, ground floor and second floor. Canavan stopped producing brooms around 1912, and a variety of businesses moved in.

In 1920, the building became one of several corner groceries in North Lawrence. First owned by the Pine brothers and then by Wiley's Grocery, it operated as such until 1960. The store was famous in the neighborhood for its penny candy. During the middle part of the twentieth century, the second floor was converted for residential use, and a one-story extension was added on the north side. When Wiley's closed, it became a shop space for a variety of service industries before falling vacant. The building has since been rehabilitated for use as commercial space on the first floor, with renovated residential space on the second.

TEEPEE JUNCTION

Junction of U.S. Highway 59 and U.S. Highway 24

Teepee Junction, located on the northern outskirts of town, is a reminder of a once great roadside attraction. Designed to resemble Native American

The grandeur of the roadside attraction Teepee Junction has deteriorated over time. At one time, the complex included a gas station, restaurant and motor court, for which the cabins, like this one, were designed to resemble teepees. *Author's collection.*

teepees, travelers could book a room and stay in this small roadside hotel. The main teepee building design was patented by its creator, Frank W. McDonald, in 1930. Most likely, this one was constructed sometime in the late 1920s, well ahead of later "Wigwam Villages" found throughout the country.

The main structure stands at fifty feet in height and thirty-three feet in diameter. It was the centerpiece of a U.S. Highway 40 roadside "Indian Village" complex that also included a gas station, a restaurant and a motor court of smaller teepee cabins. In addition to keeping up the painting schematic over the years, owners have added floodwater line markers to the building. North Lawrence quickly receives the brunt of Kansas River flooding, and markers denote floods in 1935 and 1951. Since its opening, the complex has also served as a restaurant and party venue. While the fourteen cabins have long since been demolished, you can still see the main teepee and a one-floor building with a teepee on either end.

PINKNEY

Located along a bend of the Kansas River, this area was settled as part of the original Lawrence townsite as early as 1854. Today, the modern neighborhood features several homes, businesses and parks. Once located here was a brickyard and expansive brewery, as well as the home of Lawrence Memorial Hospital, the town's first hospital.

Historic parks such as Woody Park, Robinson Park and Clinton Park reside along with newer Burcham Park, Constant Park and Sandra Shaw Park. The three-acre Clinton Park was part of the original town plat in 1854 and still features the only part of the large ravine that once stretched from the river and into West Lawrence. Structures from a 1938 neighborhood project, working with the National Youth Administration, remain. A stone wall at the other end of the neighborhood, located at 5th and Tennessee Streets, was constructed during the Great Depression by the Works Progress Administration project.

Until 1912, 6th Street was called Pinkney and then Pinckney Street. In 2020, the neighborhood reverted to its Pinkney name, as "Pinckney" was associated with Revolutionary War General Charles Cotesworth Pinckney, an outspoken defender of slavery during the Constitutional Convention. As he was a plantation owner and celebrator of the fugitive slave cause, the neighborhood chose to associate its neighborhood with William Pinkney, who gave an influential antislavery speech in 1789. The school still retains the "Pinckney" name.

Covering three acres, Clinton Park was part of the original Lawrence town plat. In 1938, several amenities were added, including several "ovens," a shelter house, a retaining wall (which still exists) and restrooms. *Author's collection.*

Unlike its neighbor to the north, Old West Lawrence, Pinkney never was home to the wealthy merchant class, and the architectural styles and massing of the two district's homes reflect that. Many of the homes, constructed between the late 1850s and 1927, are predominantly in the Folk House National and Folk Victorian styles.

ROBINSON PARK-FOUNDER'S ROCK

6 East 6th Street

Officially known as In'zhúje'waxóbe, the Shunganunga Boulder, or the Sacred Red Rock, stood here in Robinson Park from 1929 until 2023. The boulder holds a tremendous significance to the Kanza (Kaw) tribe, who hold their ancestral lands in what is now eastern Kansas. Carried by glaciers and deposited near Topeka, where the Kansas River and the Shunganunga Creek merge, the boulder became a spiritual place used for prayer, community gatherings, songs and dancing.

During the 1920s, Topeka residents wished for the stone to be removed from its location and have it placed at or near the state capitol building. However, businessmen from Lawrence managed to undercut Topeka, and in the middle of the night in 1929, the natural and cultural item became the property of the City of Lawrence. It was renamed "Founder's Rock" to honor the territorial settlers and placed in Robinson Park during the city's seventy-fifth anniversary. A plaque was affixed to the stone listing the names of the original settlers.

For years, the Kanza people expressed their desire to have it returned to them. Eventually, through the work of the city and the university, via multiple grants, the stone was finally returned. A formal ceremony was held on August 29, 2023, commemorating the return with an extension of a public apology. The stone now sits on Kaw tribal land in Morris County at the Allegawaho Memorial Heritage Park, just a short distance from Council Grove.

MARY JANE "MAMIE" DILLARD HOUSE

520 Louisiana Street

Constructed by Jesse Dillard in 1889, this Queen Anne–style house would become the home of his daughter, famous local educator Mary Jane "Mamie" Dillard. Jesse was born into slavery in Virginia sometime in 1826 or 1827. When the illiterate Dillard arrived in Lawrence in 1868, he became a respected property owner, ensuring that his daughter received the education he never got. With $500, Jesse purchased a lot here, building this two-story home. Jesse and his wife, Frances, strived for their children to receive an education, with their daughter, Mary, eventually graduating from the University of Kansas in 1896.

Mary became a teacher in the all-Black primary class at Pinckney School, where Langston Hughes was enrolled when he was about seven years old. She continued to teach and advance her own education, taking graduate courses at KU in English and special education. Following this, she became principal of Lawrence's all-Black Lincoln school in North Lawrence. Throughout her life, she advocated for women's suffrage and civil rights, being appointed in 1916 by Governor Arthur Capper as one of four delegates to the convention of the Negro National Educational Congress. She died in 1954 and is buried at Oak Hill Cemetery.

CAMERON'S BLUFF

Ravine at 5th and Louisiana Streets

Despite the fact that Hugh Cameron was almost entirely self-educated, he earned a position teaching at a private school in Washington, D.C., in 1849. While there he began lifelong friendships with the likes of Daniel Webster and Stephen Douglas, bringing him back to the nation's capital throughout his life. Following stints employed as a private school teacher, working for the U.S. Treasury Department and selling *Harper's* magazine door to door, he suffered a lung hemorrhage and decided to head west in the hopes of restoring his health.

Cameron, a staunch antislavery supporter, began walking west in 1853, briefly joining the first Emigrant Aid Societies for Lawrence before continuing his walk. He set up camp in July 1854 along a shallow bend, calling it Camp Ben Harrison. While in Kansas, he served as a justice of the peace for Lawrence, a Union soldier during the Civil War (rising to the rank of lieutenant colonel), a farmer, a ferry operator and a postmaster. Sometime in the 1870s, Cameron grew disillusioned with his own political life, choosing to become a recluse.

For the next thirty years, Cameron would live in a variety of homes, including log cabins located on the ground and in homes he built in the trees, building his most elaborate and final home in this ravine, then northwest of town. Located high in one of the maple trees, Cameron cleared and hollowed out the space below to serve as a kitchen and dining room. By the spring of 1908, he had managed to have both phone service and electricity wired to the treehouse.

Cameron, while not involved in politics himself anymore, would walk

In a city filled with unique individuals, Hugh Cameron may stand at the top of the list. Known as the Kansas Hermit, Cameron lived in a treehouse in this ravine during the latter years of his life, continuing to walk to D.C. for presidential inaugurations. *Author's collection.*

from Lawrence to Washington, D.C., every four years for the presidential inauguration. Despite his reclusive lifestyle, he softened up somewhat over the years. KU students, when learning about the Kansas Hermit, trekked over to the treehouse to seek him out. Eventually, instead of chasing them off, he loosened up, inviting them to sit with him around the campfire to tell them mostly true stories about his life. During his final year of life, which came in 1908, Cameron rode a stars and stripes–clad mule in just about any parade held in town.

PINCKNEY SCHOOL

810 West 6th Street

Lawrence's first schoolhouse came about during a meeting in the fall of 1854. A small log cabin, featuring four windows and a door, was built near this location. The Emigrant Aid Company sought to expand educational services for the new settlers, and those offerings began being held on Massachusetts Street and the Unitarian Church on Ohio Street. By 1869, more space was needed, so the old Congregational Church at Louisiana and Pinckney Streets (now 6th Street) was remodeled, with two rooms opened for school in the fall of that year.

With schools and temporary locations for education being spread throughout and becoming increasingly crowded, a substantial new school building was called for. During the 1871–72 school year, four lots on Pinckney Street were purchased for the construction site of a two-room, two-story building. The red brick building was planned as only a wing of a future larger building, which would feature four to six rooms total, growing along with the city. This building was located immediately south of the building you see today. One student of note who attended Pinckney was future Harlem Renaissance poet Langston Hughes. Segregation was a fact of life when he started the second grade in 1909.

By 1929, enrollment at Pinckney had grown exponentially, and the red brick building, despite its growth, needed to be replaced with a larger and more modern building. The new one was built directly behind the old one. Once school closed in June 1931, the old building was torn down. During the summer, the new building was finished, and it opened before the start of school that September. It too continued to grow along with the city. In

The 1930 Pinckney School replaced a smaller school building constructed in 1872. The school's library is named for Langston Hughes, an alumnus of the earlier school building. *Author's collection.*

1990, the Pinckney Library was dedicated as the Langston Hughes Library for Children. The ceremonies included the placement of markers where he lived with his grandmother and, later, family friends James and Mary Reed. Connecting the school to the south side of Sixth Street is the Pinckney Tunnel. Built in the 1950s, it was designed as a safe passageway under the busy street. It was reclaimed and improved in 2011 with improved lighting and the *Tunnel Vision* mural created by Van Go, a local social services program for at-risk youth.

THE WALKER HOME

401 Indiana Street

George Nash Walker may be one of the biggest forgotten actors in history. One of the highest-paid vaudeville actors, Walker changed the culture of entertainment for African Americans, helping pave the way for the future of Black entertainers. George developed his skills in Lawrence, leaving town in 1893 at the age of twenty, hoping to make it big in California. When he arrived, he met Bert Williams, and the two entertainers began to develop an act. At the time, Black characters often were portrayed by white actors

George "Nash" Walker, seen here around the turn of the twentieth century, was a successful vaudevillian, actor and producer. Along with Bert Williams, Walker advanced African Americans in the field of entertainment like never before. *Courtesy the Joseph Hall-J. Willis Sayre Collection of Theatrical Photographs.*

in blackface and were represented as stupid or foolish and as liars. The two named their act "Two Real Coons" and flipped that notion on its head. Williams, who was light-skinned, would don blackface, while Walker would perform without makeup, acting as a "dandy." They used intellectual humor, becoming so popular with their act that they were earning the equivalent of nearly $60,000 per week in modern-day pay.

Together, Williams and Walker changed entertainment for African Americans. The duo wrote and produced *In Dahomey*, the first all-Black Broadway musical. While not a Broadway success, it had a long run in England, including a performance in front of King Edward VII. They also purchased a building in New York City, becoming a center to develop Black performers, writers and stage technicians. The two also became some of the first artists to record dance and ragtime music. Walker built a new brick home in 1908 for his mother here on Indiana Street, the same street where he grew up. The home retains much of the original craftsmanship it featured when it was constructed. After falling ill during a tour of their play *Bandana Land* in 1909, Walker returned to Lawrence, where he died on January 8, 1911, at the age of thirty-eight. He is buried at Oak Hill Cemetery with a very simple gravestone.

S.T. ZIMMERMAN HOUSE

304 Indiana Street

Mill owner S.T. Zimmerman had this unique home built in 1870. The home faces west and backs up to the Kansas River. The style of house, Second Empire, is unique in the neighborhood. The two-story brick home sports a square tower atop a bell-cast mansard roof. It is highlighted with arched windows and wrought-iron detailing throughout the rest of the exterior of the home. There has been little alteration to the exterior of the home, another unique feature. Additionally, while the interior has been altered in certain places to remain updated for modern living, it is substantially intact. It was added to the National Register of Historic Places on September 11, 1974.

LAWRENCE MEMORIAL HOSPITAL

325 Maine Street

Lawrence Memorial Hospital has been providing care to those in Lawrence since 1921. Prior to 1919, there was no publicly owned hospital in town to care for the poor. The hospital began out of a frame house located at 3rd and Maine Streets, purchased in 1919 by the Social Service League. The organization donated the structure to the city for it to establish a hospital. The city opened the hospital on January 17, 1921, following a fundraising drive to renovate and equip the building. When it opened, the hospital had 30 beds, a maternity ward, a nursery and about a dozen doctors. They quickly began to outgrow the small facility, and in 1929, Elizabeth Miller Watkins donated $200,000 for the construction of a new 50-bed brick hospital building. Additions in 1937, 1956 and 1969 brought the number of beds to 165.

In August 1975, ground was broken for the construction of a new building that would almost entirely replace the original and bring the number of beds to two hundred. Only the 1969 addition was kept, and the old hospital building was demolished in 1999. The hospital continued to grow as it moved into the twenty-first century. Additional facilities and services were added, and expansion included a conversion of all patient rooms to private rooms, new birthing rooms, the enlargement and relocation of the emergency department and the renovation of all ICU and operating rooms. In 2023, LMH Health went into partnership with the University of Kansas Health System. This enabled it to bring in specialist care for areas including sports medicine, vascular surgery and maternal-fetal medicine.

WALRUFF BREWERY BUILDING

2nd and Maine Streets

Not much remains of the old Walruff Brewery—only one simple stone stable building standing at the end of 2nd and Maine, located near Lawrence Memorial Hospital. Joseph Walruff opened the Walruff Brewery in 1867. A fire destroyed the building, but the insurance was insufficient to rebuild the operation. He brought in his older brother, John, as an investor to rebuild a bigger and better operation. The elder Walruff brother was already a wealthy man, having worked as a locksmith and machinist in Prussia before immigrating to Kansas, where he turned to politics and banking. By 1872, John had become the sole owner of the Walruff Brewery.

Located in what was then the northwest corner of town, the Lawrence brewery facilities and beer garden covered five wooded acres. The three-story brewhouse produced two thousand barrels per year, which were then stored and aged in a network of underground tunnels beneath the property. The wooded garden included strolling peacocks, canopied tables, a fine offering of foods, a shooting gallery, swings, a bowling alley and a

Not much remains of the once sprawling Walruff Brewery except this stone stable building. At one time, the property included brewing facilities, a beer garden and underground tunnels used for storage. *Author's collection.*

croquet lawn. In what was basically a monopoly, the Walruff Brewery had agreements with more than a score of saloons and five wholesalers in town and extended its reach beyond town by utilizing the railroads.

In 1881, things started to turn south when Kansas instituted prohibition of liquor throughout the state. This prohibition was not lifted until 1948 and even continued to restrict general on-premises liquor sales until 1987. In response, John Walruff remained an active crusader against prohibition. To try to skirt the law, he marketed his product as being "for medicinal purposes only." The scheme landed him trouble with the courts, involving fees and fines, plus he fled the state on multiple occasions. However, it was a losing Supreme Court case involving Salina brewer Peter Mugler in 1887 that precipitated the end of Walruff's Brewery.

For years, the property sat vacant. In 1964, the rest of what remained of the brewery complex was leveled for the construction of a new trailer park. One stone stable building remains, located just north of Lawrence Memorial Hospital. The tunnels running under the complex also remain but are inaccessible to the public.

OREAD NEIGHBORHOOD

Lawrence's Oread neighborhood is a hodgepodge of homes and demographics and includes both the Oread Historic District and the Hancock Historic District. It's home to numerous students, faculty and university staff; rental homes, apartments and historic homes; small and large houses; a few college bars; and a handful of fraternity and sorority houses. The area has become attractive not only to individuals and families but also to landlords, developers and those looking for investment opportunities, making for a unique and at times contentious relationship between neighbors. Most of the construction here occurred between 1877 and 1945 and features a wide variety of architectural styles, such as Queen Annes, Twentieth-Century Revival Tudors and Craftsman bungalows. Closer to campus are larger Greek houses, Scholarship Halls and multi-dwelling complexes in use by students. This district contains some of the oldest homes in the city and features original brick streets, hitching posts and stone steps.

THE CASTLE TEA ROOM

1307 Massachusetts Street

The building known today as the Castle Tea Room was constructed in 1894 for local merchant and Civil War vet John N. Roberts and his wife, Emily.

The Wagon Wheel, or the Wheel, was established in 1955. Sitting on the eastern slope of Mount Oread and just a short distance from campus, the Wheel has become a student institution, with burgers, pizza and drinks on the menu. *Author's collection.*

Roberts built a fortune designing and manufacturing containers, while also becoming heavily involved not only in Lawrence business but also in politics and real estate. Roberts hired some of the best artisans he could find for the construction of the Romanesque-style home, including architect John Haskell, stonemason Joel Gustafson and the young English artist Sidney Endacott for his talent in carving. Endacott spent three months carving the mantelpieces, staircases, newel posts and a china buffet for the Roberts home before returning home to become a noted watercolor artist.

J.J. Simons, owner of the Lawrence Brick Yard, purchased the home in 1919. Simons added the castle-like garage to match his new home. After Simons lost the home during the Great Depression, the home sat empty until 1943, when the Assembly of God Church purchased the home. Its plan was to disassemble the building and utilize the stone for a new church, but that never came to fruition, as Libuse "Libby" Kriz purchased the home in 1947.

Kriz, a dietitian at KU, bought the home that July with her friend Ruth Quinlan, with the dream to open it as a tearoom. When Ruth was diagnosed only a few weeks later with a terminal illness, Libby refused to be deterred and purchased the property outright. Soon thereafter, she opened the Castle Tea Room. Libby lived in the home longer than anyone, from 1947 to 2004. Following Libby's passing in 2004, her foundation undertook a

Civil War veteran John Roberts's home reflected his status in the city as a leader in Lawrence business, politics and real estate. Today, it is known as the Castle Tea Room, a special events venue, and is home to the United Way. *Author's collection.*

historic rehabilitation project on the property that won several awards for the preservation work. The building continues to serve Lawrence as both a special events venue and as office space on the second floor for the local offices of the United Way.

EDWARD HOUSE RESIDENCE

1646 Massachusetts Street

Named after Edward House, this Queen Anne–style wood-frame house was constructed in 1894. Two additions were added, one in the 1910s and another in the 1920s, which included a one-story lean-to and a two-story section, while the decks and sun porches were added in the 1980s. Many of the original features of the home remain, but the home sits with a new roof and central A/C.

When it was constructed, it was located south of Lawrence's original boundaries but within Babcock's Enlarged Addition. There have been several prominent Lawrencians who have lived here. In 1900, Edward House lived here with his wife, Florence, and three of their children, who were in their twenties. A few years later, Thomas Robinson and his family moved into the home, followed by Carl Friends (a lumberman, banker and politician at the time and later a state senator and lieutenant governor) and Thomas Sweeney (a banker and insurance salesman) and his family. Following Sweeney's death in 1936, Henry Gwinn purchased the home, owning it from 1939 to 1942. Gwinn was KU's newly hired coach, but the team did not do well under his coaching and his contract was not renewed.

The residents living here the longest, the Belts, moved in next, living here from 1943 until 1979. When local pediatrician Terry A. Riordan purchased the home in 1983, the family made a few improvements to the home. This included the remodeling of the basement for Dr. Riordan to use as a medical office. Since they sold the house in 1995, the home has changed owners several times.

EUGENE F. GOODRICH HOUSE

1711 Massachusetts Street

Located south of downtown and just a few blocks east of the university, Eugene Goodrich's Queen Anne–style house was originally located outside the original boundaries of town. The two-and-a-half-story home was built as a single-family residential home. Goodrich built this home in Babcock's Enlarged Addition after his appointment as the Lawrence postmaster in 1889. In addition to this position, which he held until 1894, he worked as a grocer and produce shipper. William Cockins bought the home in 1911, having established the Crooked L Ranch, a huge cattle ranch, in Meade County, Kansas. By 1917, his son-in-law, William Tenney, had bought into the home as well. Tenney and his wife, Eoline M. Cockins Tenney, lived in the home until 1960.

At some point during this time, the home was divided into multiple apartments, to be used as rental space for college students. A physician couple owned the home in the late twentieth century and made substantial interior renovation. The home had been neglected so much that it was dilapidated. Only one of the home's original light fixtures survived and was able to be restored, while the dormer windows on the third story contain the only surviving original stained-glass windows. Today, it is the home of Psychological Resources Inc., a firm specializing in psychological testing for public safety applicants.

According to legend, the house is said to be haunted. Back when the house served as a rental apartment for college students, mysterious occurrences were frequent. Doors were said to fling open, while attic lights and door buzzers would go on and off. Supposedly, a terrified dog once left alone in the house tore through a second-story window to jump out of the house… he survived.

LAWRENCE FIRE STATION NO. 2

1839 Massachusetts Street

Constructed in 1932 as fires were becoming too prevalent for the smaller Lawrence Fire Department, this station is the city's oldest standing one. With windows overlooking Massachusetts Street, the building was erected at a time when the city was still transitioning from horse-drawn to motorized vehicles. The department itself was first organized in 1859 as a volunteer engine company but was disbanded in 1862 because of Civil War funding shortage. Ultimately, the department became a ten-member full-time agency in 1915. The department expanded its service delivery with an emergency medical response program in 1950, which would then call for a new and additional station, this one located downtown and constructed in 1955.

However, with the new building in 1955, the days were numbered for Station No. 2. Its last fire trucks were removed from the station in the 1960s. For many years, the county ambulance service was housed here. In 1997, the department combined its emergency response force with the Douglas County Ambulance Service to create the Lawrence-Douglas County Fire Medical Department. Shift commanders would continue to use the building until 2006, and then it was used for the department's investigations unit.

In 2017, renovations began for the 1955 Station No. 1, causing its ambulance crew to relocate. Prior to that, this brick station, which retained its original wood floors and one of two original fire poles, saw some work as well. That included renovating an apartment, a full kitchen, a bathroom and private bedrooms in the second store. Framed historic photos were added, and a newer chrome pole replaced the original brass one. For a short time, the station was alive nearly as much as it was when it opened.

GEORGE AND FLORA MACKIE HOUSE

1941 Massachusetts Street

This home, owned by entrepreneur George Mackie, was constructed in the Neoclassical Revival style in 1917. It serves as a unique landmark showcasing the Mackie family's wealth. George worked in the coal mining and banking industries (albeit all outside Lawrence) during the late 1800s and early 1900s, America's Second Industrial Revolution. He arrived in the United States in 1869 from Scotland with his parents, David and Elizabeth. The family lived in Wisconsin and Illinois before settling in Kansas in 1883. David worked for the Keith and Perry Coal Company, and his son followed in his footsteps. He founded the family-owned George K. Mackie Fuel Company in 1906, developing the company as one of the region's most technologically advanced coal companies.

Mackie commissioned architect H. Alexander Drake to build the extravagant home for the family. Mackie lived in the home with his wife, Flora Bush, and their five children. Following his death in the summer of 1928, the family remained, finally selling the home in 1937 to the Lawrence Women's Club. From then until 1975, the club owned the house, sharing it temporarily during the late 1940s with the university, which used the space as women's student housing. Tensions between the two groups would eventually come to a head, causing the university to quit using it for housing. When the Lawrence Women's Club dissolved, it sold the house back into private ownership in 1975.

PRIESTLY HOUSE

1510 Kentucky Street

Following Quantrill's Raid, the city of Lawrence experienced a period of growth. In addition to rebuilding, additional business and the Lawrence-Leavenworth-Galveston Railroad's arrival, Lawrence saw the formation of the university atop Mount Oread. Developers in town pounced on the growth and began building homes as a speculative endeavor at the end of the Civil War. The Priestly House, constructed around 1864, was likely a part of this growth. William Priestly, captain of the 93rd Ohio Volunteers during the war, moved his family to Lawrence from nearby Baldwin City in 1872, purchasing the home that April. The reason for the move was so his children could attend KU. His daughter, Cassie Priestly Yates, became one of the first women to graduate from the university.

When the Panic of 1873 hit, followed by a drought and grasshopper infestation, the Priestlys stayed—even though nearly one thousand other residents would leave during the mid- to late 1870s. Members of the Priestly family would own and reside in the home for more than one hundred years, selling it in 1986. Lawrence Preservation Alliance purchased the home when it came up for demolition. In 1987, it sold the home to William Haw, who agreed to refrain from making alterations or improvements without prior approval.

BENEDICT HOUSE

923 Tennessee Street

The Benedict House stands within the original townsite of Lawrence, which was platted in 1854. Constructed in the Late Victorian Stick style around 1869, this home has seen several additions and renovations throughout time. The original frame building was only about forty by forty-five feet, while the more modern metal-clad addition in the rear, along with the gable-front addition, dates to 1882.

James A. Bell, a carpenter, constructed this home. At that time, the 900 block of Tennessee Street showcased only eight homes. The neighborhood would grow to twelve homes by 1880 and an additional eight by 1912. This home, however, was sold a few times before Sarah and Frank Benedict bought it in 1873. They owned the property for decades.

Following Frank Sr.'s death in 1930, the family sold the home to Esther Ragle, who lived there until her death in 1977. For a decade after, the home served as a rental property, divided into two apartments, before ultimately being purchased by the Lawrence Preservation Alliance. Its certified rehabilitation project, which took place in the 1980s and 1990s, removed most of the nonhistorical additions made to the home following 1891.

COLONEL JAMES C. BLOOD HOUSE

1015 Tennessee Street

Colonel James Clinton Blood, the first mayor of Lawrence, constructed one of the oldest buildings still standing in town. Blood was a major player in establishing Lawrence and became heavily involved in the Free State militia throughout the Bleeding Kansas era. He also served as a local businessman and lawyer.

Colonel Blood came to the territory in 1854, serving as an agent for Amos A. Lawrence, who then was both the treasurer of the New England Emigrant Aid Society and the city's benefactor. Lawrence sent Blood and Charles Branscomb to explore the region abutting Missouri's western border to select a suitable location for the Free State parties to settle in. Once they chose their site, which is now Lawrence, the duo traveled back to Kansas City to meet arriving emigrants, leading them to this location on August 1, 1854—the birth of Lawrence.

Blood would go on to become the city's first mayor on July 31, 1857, and served as a delegate to the Wyandotte Constitutional Convention in 1859. That same year, he was elected to the board of trustees for the proposed "Lawrence University." By the time the school was finally realized, the Civil War had passed and it had become the University of Kansas. He would also serve as the county treasurer from 1864 to 1868 and was elected to the state legislature in 1869. Blood's home was purchased sometime in the early 1880s by J.B. Shearer. To this day, the home remains a private residence and is one of the more splendiferous homes in town. In 1972, it was added to the National Register of Historic Places.

GEORGE AND ANNIE BELL HOUSE

1008 Ohio Street

George Bell, Douglas County clerk at the time, bought an empty lot on the eastern slope of Mount Oread in October 1862 for a total of sixty dollars. While he was serving as the county clerk, Bell had this locally quarried limestone house built over the next year. It stands as one of the oldest homes in Lawrence, consisting of four rooms and containing a central chimney.

During Quantrill's Raid, George Bell, when he heard of the town being attacked, left the home to assist in protecting the town. Unfortunately, the raiders attempted to burn down the house, with the family managing to save the home; as he left home, he told Mrs. Bell that "they might kill" him but that they could not kill the principles they stood for. During his absence from home, George Bell lost his life.

George and Annie Bell lived in this home, built during 1862–63. When raiders arrived on August 21, 1863, George left to protect the town. While his family managed to save the home from being burned, George lost his life during the melee. *Author's collection.*

The Bell House was occupied by Annie and their six children (the youngest only two years old at the time) off and on for several years following George's death. Frequently, the remaining family members would live in the cellar of the home, renting out the upstairs rooms to boarders. Additionally, Annie would earn her living by setting up a restaurant above the local drugstore. When the family moved out, John and Mary Allison moved in; they would own the home for nearly five decades starting in 1914. In the early 1980s, restoration began in earnest, and by 1983, their work had placed the property in the National Register of Historic Places. The home continues to be utilized as a private residence but stands as a great example of the territorial period.

GOVERNOR ROBINSON'S 1856 HOME SITE

1115 Louisiana Street

In 1854, Governor Robinson served as the official financial agent to Eli Thayer's New England Emigrant Aid Company. In June, he and Charles Branscomb scouted out eastern Kansas to find suitable land where the company could establish a settlement dedicated to the Free State cause. He would lead the first two companies to the new settlement, building his home along the slope of Mount Oread. He angered many with his passionate support of the Free Staters, in opposition to the proslavery advocates. He was illegally elected territorial governor of Kansas in January 1856.

In May 1856, Robinson's home was burned to the ground, as he had previously been arrested for the crime of treason by Sheriff Samuel Jones. From that spring until September, Robinson and other Free State leaders, including John Brown Jr., were held in Camp Sackett near Lecompton. All that remains to remember the location of this home is a small granite marker in the grass off the sidewalk.

HANDEL T. MARTIN HOUSE

1709 Louisiana Street

Handel Tong Martin immigrated to the United States from England, settling in Logan County, Kansas, in 1886. Possessing only a country school education until the age of thirteen, he came out of his education with a deep interest in the burgeoning field of vertebrate paleontology. His career included exploring and collecting fossils for Professor O.C. Marsh at Yale, collecting and sending specimens to the leading museums in the United States and Europe and working at the American Museum of Natural History's paleontology lab in the winter of 1894, before going to work at KU in 1896 as Samuel Williston's chief assistant and preparator. His work can be found in the Smithsonian and the London Museum of Natural History. As KU's curator of fossil vertebrates from 1912 to 1931, he helped KU gain a reputation as one of the nation's best natural history museums, a status it continues to hold, now as part of the Biodiversity Institute.

Originally, Handel and his family lived in a home in an older residential neighborhood west of downtown. In 1917, the subdivision of University Place, located south of campus, was being developed, and the family moved into this new American Foursquare home built the previous year. Boarding with the Martins were Hazel, an assistant KU librarian; a nurse named Hattie; and a gentleman named Harry. Martin was not the only prominent person to live here. In the early 1960s, Charles Bradford Black owned the home. Black was a talented KU basketball player who played five seasons in the NBA. He was also a World War II hero for the U.S. Army Air Corps, being awarded the Distinguished Flying Cross. At KU, he became the only four-time All-American, the first Jayhawk to be named All-Conference four times and the first to score one thousand points in his college career.

DOWNTOWN

The downtown district of Lawrence has been the heart of the city since the founding of the settlement in 1854. A.D. Searle, one of the early settlers through the New England Emigrant Aid Company, prepared the plan for the town of Lawrence in 1854. Searle laid out the city in a grid system of streets measuring eighty feet in width. There were three exceptions—three major thoroughfares that were planned to connect blocks that he reserved for public uses, such as parks and a future college. One of these streets was Massachusetts Street (best known locally as Mass Street), and each of the three were one hundred feet wide. It is flanked to the west by Vermont Street and to the east by New Hampshire Street; it is bordered on the north by 6th Street and runs north to South Park Street.

The city was nearly destroyed twice—once by Sheriff Samuel Jones in May 1856 and then again on the morning of August 21, 1863, by William Quantrill and his band of guerrillas. During the rebuilding process that followed the latter raid, from 1864 to 1873, sixty-one of the extant buildings in downtown were constructed—a vast majority along the 700 and 800 blocks of Massachusetts. During this period, only stone or brick buildings were permitted along the main drag because of the danger of fire in such closely packed buildings. While entertainment, menus and retail preferences have changed over the years, downtown Lawrence's business offerings haven't changed too terribly much.

William Quantrill and his rebel guerrillas destroyed a large portion of Lawrence and murdered hundreds of men and boys on the morning of August 21, 1863, depicted here in a September 5, 1863 sketching of the massacre from *Harper's Weekly. Courtesy of the Library of Congress.*

FREE STATE BREWING COMPANY

636 Massachusetts Street

This is the brewery that brought a century of lost liquor back to the state of Kansas. When Chuck Magerl opened Free State Brewing in 1989, he took over a neglected but historic spot in downtown Lawrence. The brewery is located where a wood-frame shack housed the railroad car shed of the Kaw Valley Interurban Railway in the early twentieth century and later served as the transportation hub for all bus traffic in town. Adjacent to the building, located at 638 Mass, was the former Kaw Valley Interurban Station, constructed in 1912 and now housing the popular La Prima Tazza coffee shop.

Magerl's background in biology, engineering and history, along with a passion for changing Kansas's blue laws, led to changes in beer sales and manufacturing in Kansas. Add this to his own family tree—he had a grandfather who spent time in Leavenworth prison for bottling liquor during Prohibition—and the recipe has been successful. The original

In 1989, Chuck Magerl's Free State Brewery led to changes in beer sales and manufacturing throughout the state. Housed in part of the old Kaw Valley Interurban Railway car shed, the brewery has served as a hotbed of activity for more than thirty-five years. *Author's collection.*

fourteen-barrel brewhouse has since expanded from the brewery and restaurant on Mass Street, as well as a bottling/canning/shipping facility built in East Lawrence.

Additionally, in September 1856, Lawrence faced the threat of an invading force of more than 2,500 Missouri ruffians under the command of David Rice Atchison and John W. Reid. Sheriff Samuel Jones had sacked the town just four months earlier, and they sought to finish the job. The townspeople grabbed what arms they could find and gathered between two circular earthen forts on Mass Street. Present that day, and heavily armed, was abolitionist and captain of the Liberty Guards John Brown. As this ad hoc leader realized, the group needed motivation, and he clambered on top of a dry goods box, about twenty-five feet west of Free State Brewing, in the middle of the street and gave an address on tactics to more than one hundred armed citizens, just steps from the front door of the brewery.

LIBERTY HALL

642–644 Massachusetts Street

Prior to holding Liberty Hall, the space on the corner of 7th and Massachusetts was well known as the home to the abolitionist newspaper the *Herald of Freedom*, first published on January 6, 1855. Publisher George Washington Brown had previously garnered the support of the Massachusetts Emigrant Aid Company. Later that year, the building was sacked and burned, and the press was thrown in the Kansas River, as it was deemed a nuisance to proslavery advocates by Douglas County Sheriff Samuel Jones. In its place, Samuel Edwin Poole constructed a building that housed the city post office and a retail operation that sold sewing machines, pianos and

This site was once the home for the abolitionist newspaper the *Herald of Freedom*, the city post office, a retail establishment, the Bowersock Opera House and the *Lawrence Journal* newspaper. It's also been known by a number of other names before finally settling on Liberty Hall. *Author's collection.*

organs. Unfortunately, this iteration was destroyed as well, this time during Quantrill's Raid.

In 1870, the rebuilt structure was christened Liberty Hall, suggested by Reverend E.D. Bentley, who heard future president Abraham Lincoln call Lawrence the "Cradle of Liberty." During the 1880s, the building was redesigned to serve as a gathering place for town meetings and political debates, including a visit by author Oscar Wilde. From 1882 to 1911, the hall served as Bowersock's Opera House and housed the operations of the *Lawrence Journal* newspaper. Following a disastrous fire, J.D. Bowersock added an additional floor and the now signature Beaux Arts–style architecture when a reconstruction project to make the building fireproof began in 1912. At this point, Bowersock converted the space into a movie theater, showing its first sound film in 1927.

Throughout the years, the building has been known as the Dickinson Theater, the Jayhawker Theater, the Red Dog Inn Night Club and Bugsy's before finally resting with the current iteration, Liberty Hall Cinema, which returned in 1986. It has operated as such ever since and hosts concerts, speeches, movies and special occasions; it has also contained a video store that far outlasted its chain competitors. Much of the building's original décor from the 1920s has been retained, including the original balcony area.

ELDRIDGE HOTEL

701 Massachusetts Street

With the passage of the Kansas-Nebraska Act, abolitionists in Boston, Massachusetts, created the New England Emigrant Aid Company. Their goal was to bring antislavery immigrants to the new territory, hoping to ensure the passage of Kansas as a Free State in the Union. When company agents arrived in Lawrence, they erected a temporary way station for travelers, naming it the Free State Hotel. It quickly became a major site for the political movement in Lawrence and a target for those opposing them.

On May 21, 1856, Douglas County Sheriff Samuel J. Jones gathered a large group of proslavery men. They arrived to sack the town of Lawrence, tossing the newspaper press into the river, terrorizing the townspeople and burning the Free State Hotel. Following the disaster, Shalor Eldridge built a new hotel in its place, naming it the Eldridge

The Eldridge House's post-raid structure is seen here in 1867, standing one more story higher than the last out of defiance by owner Shalor Eldridge. *Courtesy of the Library of Congress.*

House. In response, he built it up to three stories, one story higher than the previous iteration. This hotel stood until Quantrill arrived in 1863 and was burned it to the ground once again. Eldridge stepped forth, building another hotel in its place and again adding another story in defiance. It was finished in 1866 by George W. Deitzler.

Refurbished in 1925, Eldridge's third hotel lasted as such for nearly a century before being converted into apartments in 1970. During a downtown resurgence in the 1980s, the Eldridge was again retrofitted and reopened as a hotel. In 2004, a new group of investors purchased the hotel, restoring it back to the 1925 version and opening it the following year. One guest may continue to roam the halls of the hotel: Shalor Eldridge. Apparently, his favorite location to be is room 506. The hotel features a restaurant, bar, event space and spa.

RUDY'S PIZZERIA

704 Massachusetts Street

Constructed in 1870, this site has seen a variety of businesses take up residence here—office space, barbershop, car dealership, auto repair shop and retail.

By the turn of the century and continuing on well into the early twentieth century, the building was home to a number of legal, real estate and medical offices, including a law firm operated by Joseph Riggs and William Sinclair, who by 1888 were the only ones with office space in the building. As such, the building would become synonymous with Sinclair's name.

However, with the prevalence of automobiles emerging by the mid-1910s, automotive business began to move in, and by the 1920s, automotive services had become the primary tenants. In 1927, the building was expanded and remodeled to house an auto repair shop on one half of the lot. By the 1950s, insurance and real estate had moved back in, with Hemphill Realty remaining in the building for decades. In 1970, they were the main business in the upper part of the building. Downstairs, H.A.A.S. Furniture operated from 1972 to 1974 before a design company owned by Bob Gould and Dave Evans opened its offices in the space.

A massive fire in the late 1970s led to the restoration of the building. The main floor was converted into restaurant space in 1984, which it has remained since. One of the long-standing restaurants, since 2002, is Chad Glazer's Rudy's Pizzeria, accessed by a short set of steps down below street level. In 2012, the building was renovated to become more modernized, changing out the wood for steel so another fire wouldn't destroy the building. Despite these changes, the exterior has changed very little.

FORMER *LAWRENCE DAILY JOURNAL-WORLD* OFFICES

722 Massachusetts Street

This building was constructed in 1866 to house J.G. Sands's saddlery and harness shop, Sands & Company, which operated elsewhere prior to the raid and operated here until 1896. Following a brief occupation by Boener Brothers' wholesale cigar factory, the *Lawrence Daily Journal-World* took over the space, remaining until 1954, when it moved just off Massachusetts Street to a larger facility.

Between 1905 and 1912, newspaper president, editor and business manager W.C. Simons had the building entirely remodeled. In 1912, the façade was reconstructed to be two feet taller, and the addition of another story extended the building farther back. Simons would eventually buy the deed to the building in 1923. He had it altered again in 1927 to make for more room. About a decade after the newspaper moved locations, Chet and Mary Johnson's Chet Johnson Furniture Company moved in. Opening in 1964, their furniture became a staple of downtown shopping for more than thirty-five years, before closing in 1999. Additional retail operations have operated here since.

MILLER'S HALL

723–725 Massachusetts Street

Construction on Miller's Hall, built for Free State Party activist Josiah Miller, commenced sometime in the late 1850s and was finished in stages. Despite this, the building resembles a single structure from the outside. Starting out as a small, one-story limestone building in 1856–58, the following year, a two-story structure was added to the south and east of the original one. In 1858, when construction was finalized on the addition, a three story-building was added to the front of the one-story structure at 723 Massachusetts. A third story was added to the two-story 725 Massachusetts structure in 1863.

This daguerreotype of abolitionist John Brown is thought to have been taken during his time living in Kansas around 1856. *Courtesy of the Boston Athenaeum.*

The original business, located on the first floor, belonged to Miller's general mercantile store and David Prager's jewelry store. The second floor served as residences, and the third story was used as a meeting hall, playing an important role in Lawrence and the formation of Kansas. For a few days, the hall served as the first state capitol, but more notably as headquarters of the Free State Party, the home of the Kansas Free State organization, the Grand Army of the Republic headquarters and as meetings for the Masons, the Presbyterian Church and the Turnverein, a German immigrant organization. Miller operated his store here for a decade, as well as serving as publisher for the *Kansas Free Press* and as the first probate judge of the county in 1857. The building remained in the family until 1889.

It was upstairs, in the meeting hall, where John Brown gave his "Shirt of Blood" speech, stating, "The crimes of this guilty land will never be purged away but with blood." While partially destroyed during Quantrill's Raid, the structure's reconstruction was completed in 1864, becoming one of only two buildings downtown that managed to mostly survive the raid. Once the Millers sold the building, it served as a variety of business operations. The 723 building would house primarily grocery stores and confectioneries throughout the 1930s. Later, a bookstore and jewelry stores would inhabit this building. Goldmaker's Jewelry has been one of its longest-serving tenants since that time.

THE HOUSE BUILDING

729–731 Massachusetts Street

Located in the center of downtown Lawrence and constructed during the pivotal territorial period by Josiah Miller from 1858 to 1860, the House Building is one of the oldest and most important historical buildings, constructed following Sheriff Jones's 1856 raid on the town. Miller was one of five Lawrence business owners who petitioned the federal government for redress following the sheriff's sack. Miller's building served as home for his commercial business and a popular meeting place for antislavery advocates. As a leading figure in the New England Emigrant Aid Company's effort to attract settlers to the territory, his name, new position of postmaster and business began drawing attention. In 1860, Miller added another identical building to the north half of the lot, creating a fifty-foot-wide frontage known as the "Miller Block." In 1862, Miller leased out the southern half of the building to Jacob House for his new gentleman's clothing store.

During Quantrill's Raid, House was in this building and forced at gunpoint to serve as a local guide for the raiders. In return, his life was spared, but this led to the deaths of many townspeople and the destruction of numerous buildings. At that time, the commercial district only ran from 6th to 9th Street along Massachusetts. The House building was the sole structure left standing on this block and one of only four commercial buildings to survive that fateful August morning. Undeterred, House continued to operate his store, the St. Louis Clothing Store, until his death in 1913. Following the death of House, his son, Robert, took over the business, then considered to be the oldest clothing merchant in the state at that time. When Robert died, his wife, Irma, inherited the business. Irma remodeled the building, adding office space in a second story in the early 1920s. During the remodeling, she had the third story removed, added the offices and had the name "HOUSE" added to the second-story façade, which can still be seen. Over the years, the Miller Block has housed clothing stores, a music shop, Clarence "Swede" Wilson's billiard parlor, offices for lawyers and dentists, a furniture store and an African American lodge.

JEFFERSON'S

743 Massachusetts Street

Jefferson's, a longtime favorite sports bar and grill, has been located here for a number of years, but previously this building has seen multiple businesses occupy both the streets and upper floors. Not long after the end of the Civil War, in 1866, the W.H.R. Lykins Bank opened here, followed by the National Bank of Lawrence, then Steinberg & Brothers Dry Goods until 1888. The longest tenant here was the Fair Dry Goods Store, which opened in January 1890 and remained here for nearly four decades, closing in 1928. Multiple retailers and clothiers would operate out of the building for multiple decades.

During the 1950s and 1960s, Lawrence's only African American lawyer, Leroy Harris, took out the office upstairs. One night, in 1958, Philip A. Johnson walked into Harris's office and shot him to death, minutes later walking down the street to the police station to turn himself in. Following the incident, the upstairs office was sealed off and unused, followed by further inaccessibility because of a gas leak in 1977, until it was reopened during a fire in 2015 that revealed its existence. The downstairs portion of the building, since the late 1980s, has housed several restaurants, with Jefferson's moving in during June 2000. A 2024 renovation to the building removed the corrugated metal storefront on the upper levels of the building, which also meant the removal of the patch that once covered Harris's office.

MERCHANT'S FIRST NATIONAL BANK

746 Massachusetts Street

Constructed in March 1932, this building first served as Lawrence's First National Bank. Since that time, the bank building has also served as office space for KU's Film School and, most recently, as a series of restaurants. Mystery also surrounds the bank as a potential early bank robbery site. The bank looks very much the same as when it was constructed, especially on the outside. Aside from modern upgrades to serve as a restaurant, not much has changed in the appearance of the interior either. Not long after the bank opened its doors, it welcomed its most infamous guests.

Clyde Barrow, accompanied by Ralph Fults and Raymond Hamilton, had been up north, where the weather was impeding their operations. Deciding to head south, they stopped in Lawrence, finding rooms at the Eldridge Hotel. They scoped out the bank and monitored the movements of bank president William Docking. Finding Docking's arrival time to be beneficial, Barrow and Fults entered the bank with shotguns, while Hamilton kept the

It is quite possible that Clyde Barrow, Ralph Fults and Raymond Hamilton stopped in Lawrence in March 1932 to rob this bank, home to Lawrence's First National Bank. While the structure is now a restaurant, the event is commemorated with a picture of Clyde near the bathroom, housed in the original bank vault. *Author's collection.*

car running at the corner. Their take was $33,000 (nearly $500,000 today). Controversy surrounds the event because there is no actual concrete evidence that it ever even happened, but the lack of the FDIC at the time, meaning bank deposits were not federally insured against loss, could have caused a run on the bank, causing panic, thus the silence. Regardless, the site honors Clyde Barrow and the robbery with a picture of him near the bathroom, which once served as the original bank vault.

LEO A. BEUERMAN MARKER

746 Massachusetts Street

Lawrence is a city well known for its characters, with an eclectic bunch of people having resided here. One such person, memorialized by a plaque, is Leo A. Beuerman, noted as a "Distinguished Citizen of Lawrence." Leo faced limitations from his birth in 1902: he was deaf, unable to walk, went blind and at his tallest stood thirty-six inches in height. However, he would not be deterred. To maneuver around town, he utilized a handmade cart. Leo would bring the cart to town on a tractor that he had rigged with a series of chains and pulleys. Once downtown, he would sell pencils and small objects in the hopes of remaining self-sufficient but also to help others in need. Gene Boomer, in 1969, directed a short documentary film featuring Leo. It was nominated for an Academy Award for Best Documentary Short. Following his death in 1974, Leo was buried at Oak Hill Cemetery.

ROUND CORNER DRUG

801 Massachusetts Street

Round Corner Drug operated at this location for nearly 150 years. Originally Woodward and Company, the drugstore was founded by B.W. Woodward in 1855; he occupied this building, as it was constructed specifically for his pharmacy around 1865–66. Woodward moved his operation to this location after having been housed in the Eldridge House hotel until Quantrill's Raid. In 1897, Woodward retired, closing his pharmacy. Within three years, on

A drugstore has operated in this location since the Civil War, with Round Corner Drugs being housed here for nearly 150 of those years. The drugstore closed in 2009, and since then, the site has been home to a series of restaurants. *Author's collection.*

October 19, 1900, B.W. Woodward died. Five years later, the building was remodeled; a two-story storage room in the back of the building was added. The drugstore was reopened in 1914 by R.G. Eyth and Walter Varrnum following nearly seventeen years of dormancy. The partners renamed the operation Round Corner Drug. In 1922, when George Lowman bought a one-third interest in the company, they announced plans to remodel the store, which would come in 1926. Over much of the next century, despite changing owners a handful of times, the drugstore business continued to operate. In 1984, Tom Wilcox purchased both the pharmacy operation and building, operating the business until 2009.

Following the closure of Round Corner Drug on July 8, 2009, it has served as home to a small number of restaurants. In 2016, Bret Springs and Zach Martin opened RND Corner Grill, following a total overhaul of the building. Despite this, the renovations managed to keep its historic appearance and atmosphere and added a mural depicting downtown Lawrence in 1911. Upstairs, 801½ Massachusetts has been home to several different offices, J.D. Patterson's dentist office, galleries, small businesses and a feminist bookstore over the years. In the back addition, which is now a restaurant kitchen, a popular cheese shop operated from the 1980s until the early 2000s.

RIDENOUR-BAKER BUILDING

802–804 Massachusetts Street

Peter Ridenour and Harlow Baker arrived in Lawrence at about the same time in 1858, both newly married and residing temporarily in the Whitney House. They decided to go into the grocery business together, purchasing this lot and procuring a contract to build a store. They would later expand their grocery business into a wholesale and retail operation, one of the few in the West. Their building was destroyed during Quantrill's Raid, but they were undaunted; this structure was one of the first to be rebuilt, restocked and reopened to the public. When the duo moved their operation to Kansas City, Friedo Barteldes became the proprietor of the store, adding seed packets to his grocery operation. The success of the seed packets led Friedo to convert his business into the Kansas Seed House, the largest of its kind west of the

Today home to the popular Sunflower Outdoor & Bike Shop, the Ridenour & Baker building was destroyed during Quantrill's Raid. The duo rebuilt their grocery business, becoming one of the first to reopen to the public. It later housed the Barteldes Seed Company, where a young Langston Hughes sold collected seeds. *Author's collection.*

Mississippi. As a young man, poet Langston Hughes would collect seeds and sell them at the back dock to the company.

Friedo's nephew, F.W. Barteldes, joined the business in 1874, taking it over with Max Wilhelmi when Friedo died in 1887. Fire struck the building in 1904, and the Barteldes family rebuilt again, this time fireproof and with an additional story. In 1906, the company was incorporated as the Barteldes Seed Company, expanding to Denver and Oklahoma City, with headquarters relocated to Denver in 1961.

In 1972, Dave and Susan Millstein founded Sunflower Surplus, a retail business encouraging people to get outdoors. Following a short stint on Vermont Street, the Millsteins moved their operations here. Originally an Army-Navy surplus store, it has become Sunflower Outdoor & Bike Shop, one of the leading businesses of its kind. Fire couldn't slow them down either, but it did disrupt business when the shop was ravaged in February 1997. The store relocated for one year, after which the shop reopened in this location. In 2002, longtime staffer Dan Hughes and his wife, Karla, bought the building from the Millsteins, further cementing the business's place in the community. Sunflower has expanded to include more outdoor activities, the addition of a café and pub in 2002 and a wellness studio in 2023.

THE CASBAH BUILDING

803 Massachusetts Street

Constructed in 1866 during the rebuilding of downtown following the Civil War, this building housed Urbansky Dry Goods, followed by several other iterations of the same business. The upstairs, during the 1870s, was occupied by physicians who also lived in the building. Following that, the building housed a dentist's office upstairs and a books and stationery store on the main floor for roughly two decades before becoming home to the first university bookstore. It operated for four decades in this location from 1896 to 1936. The building was converted back into usage as a dry goods store until the mid-1970s, operating under a few different owners until 1974, such as Jeffries Dry Goods and Terrill's Dry Goods.

After sitting vacant for a short time, the Casbah moved in in 1976. When the Casbah opened its doors, the space used the name Sunflower International, being composed of multiple shops and restaurants, including an arts and crafts store, a gift shop and silversmith shop, with a glassware manufacturing store opening upstairs in 1980 and an art gallery in 1990. The name Sunflower International was dropped in 1997 when the business sold; however, it kept the Casbah name while operating its retail business. The Casbah, as a retail establishment, closed in 2007 and was replaced the following year with a healthy and organic grocery store called the Casbah Market. It lasted a few years, with the Burger Stand moving from its location on 623 Vermont to the Casbah space in 2010.

NEWMARK BUILDING

809 Massachusetts Street

Constructed just after the end of the Civil War in 1865 and modified in 1912, this two-story brick building features a glass recessed center entry with large display windows. Above the windows is a stone plaque carved with "1855 Newmark's 1912," sporting both the dates of Lawrence's founding and the building's remodel date. Several businesses have called the Newmark Building home over the years.

The Newmark Building, constructed just after the Civil War, today is home to the famed Raven Book Store, which was founded in 1987. The bookstore moved to this historic building in 2021. *Author's collection.*

Following a massive electrical fire in October 2018, the building was restored and rehabilitated to maintain its historical character. They managed to restore the limestone façade on the back of the building, including two original windows; most of the original wood floors on the first and second floor; and the first floor's original tin ceiling. With the project completed, Raven Book Store relocated from its smaller location off 7th Street on the main floor here, while the upstairs was converted into two one-bedroom apartments. The Raven is an independent, employee-owned bookstore founded in 1987 and was *Publisher's Weekly* 2022 Bookstore of the Year.

MARKS JEWELERS

817 Massachusetts Street

The building located here was constructed sometime in the mid-1860s, following Quantrill's Raid. In the beginning, 817 Massachusetts housed a variety of commercial operations, including a clothier, a grocery store and tobacco shops. In 1880, Sol Marks opened his jewelry store here. His son, Julius Marks, took over when Sol passed away in 1934 and then sold the business to Delbert Eisele in 1961. Julius retired, selling to Eisele, a watchmaker who had worked for both Sol and Julius. When Delbert bought the business, it was said to be the oldest family-owned business of its kind in the state. Now, Marks stands as one of the oldest jewelry stores in the United States.

LOVE GARDEN SOUNDS

822 Massachusetts Street

Sometime following Quantrill's 1863 raid on Lawrence, this building was constructed and housed a saddle and harness shop. While the date of its construction is currently unknown, the first mention of the building in the city directory came in 1868–69. A.W. Apitz and his son, Frederick, operated the store before transferring it to Charles Apitz in 1886. Apitz moved the business next door, and Achning's Hardware moved in, selling hardware, farm machinery, sporting goods and cutlery. Father and son owners Charles Aching and Charles Jr. were also members of the Lawrence Turnverein, becoming influential members of Lawrence's German American community.

Following his father's death in 1910, Charles Jr. became the sole proprietor of the hardware store, which continued to remain in this location until 1972. That same year, this building became home to Trader's Pawn Shop, operating in the location until 1984, after which it sat vacant until 1990. Love Garden Sounds, which opened in the 900 block of Massachusetts during the early 1990s, moved to this location in 2009 and remains in business today. This music store, with a vast collection of records, has managed to maintain much of the building's original architecture, including the original flooring and a large stone structure that may have served once as a fireplace.

WIEDEMANN BUILDING

835 Massachusetts Street

William Wiedemann operated a confectionery store in Lawrence from 1868. Upon his death in 1879, his son, William, took over operations. He moved the store to 835 Massachusetts in 1886, brandishing the Wiedemann's name until the 1940s. When he moved the store, he kept the soda fountain concept his father added but jettisoned the toy business that had once proved successful. In its early years, the ice cream was made outside the rear of the store and was frozen by literal horsepower—a horse hitched to the ice cream freezer would walk rounds as the ice was frozen.

The popular candy and ice cream store served as a prominent social center, dance hall and tearoom. The store stood out as something special, and its vanilla ice cream and boxed candied chocolates were raved about. The store itself was large, running seventy-five feet to the back. Tiny tiles made up the floor, with a long fountain and high stools running along the store's right. On the left was the office and cashier's cage, with candy counters filling out the rest. Upstairs is where the Wiedemanns lived. His daughter, Louise, taught piano there.

Richard Wagstaff purchased the building in the winter of 1920, adding the popular Tea Room & Grill on the second floor. Both floors became a popular meeting place for local organizations, university students and clubs, as well as a popular dance hall. Weidemann's continued to operate until 1943. John Parker had just purchased the operation when World War II struck, and he had to go off to war. Supplies became more difficult to purchase, and Wiedemann's was sold at auction. From 1952 to 1989, the building housed the Jay Shoppe, a women's fashion store. It continues to operate as a retail establishment to this day.

WEAVER'S DEPARTMENT STORE

901 Massachusetts Street

This locally owned and operated department store has stood in this space since 1857 and remains the oldest retail establishment in town. Weaver's features apparel for men, women and children, as well as shoes, bedding, kitchenware, gifts and cosmetics. To provide some comparison, Macy's Department Store was established in 1858, one year younger than Weaver's. The operation was founded in 1857 by Lathrop Bullene. He hired A.D. Weaver as his partner for the operation in 1883, following Weaver's marriage to Bullene's daughter. His son-in-law purchased the store soon after the wedding, and the operation adopted the Weaver name in 1886. Brady Ellery, today's president of Weaver, is a third-generation owner/operator and had risen to president in 2019, following his participation in the business in 2012.

The current Weaver's building was constructed in 1911. On four floors, Weaver's covers twenty thousand square feet and employs roughly fifty employees covering several departments. To this day, these employees continue to use the pneumatic tube system that was installed when constructed. The store continues to draw shoppers downtown. Additionally, the city's real Santa Claus can be found here. As part of the city's annual Holiday Lighting Ceremony, Old Saint Nick shows up on Weaver's roof and is then allowed to be rescued by the city fire department and its ladder truck.

DRAKE'S BAKERY

907 Massachusetts Street

Constructed in the late 1860s, by 1868, this address was home to John Boyer's Meat Market. It continued to remain a meat market for several years, but in 1872, there was some upheaval. Boyer, on December 18, 1872, got into a drunken argument with a Mr. Akin. Following this, he locked himself in his home as his wife and children fled, refusing to be arrested. A butchery operated by L. Hardwick and James Doak moved in after, offering a variety of meats, including dried buffalo. By 1885, the building housed a clothing store and then a millinery in 1888. It would return as a meat market and grocery store until 1905, when a billiard hall moved in for a short period. The building was up for sale the following year.

In 1906, the New Nickel Theater moved in. Here, visitors could see new motion pictures for five cents. Also housed here was the Lawrence Undertaking Company. The Oread replaced the New Nickel Theater from 1910 to 1915, after which a series of bakeries occupied the space, including Drake's Bakery, starting in 1927. Drake's remained a Lawrence institution for more than five decades. Carl Drake ran the shop with his wife, Ruth, and brother, Jay. Fruitcakes became their specialty during World War II because of their ability to be sent overseas to troops and long shelf life. Carl's son, Joseph, operated the business following his dad's death in 1988. Since that time, the Mad Greek restaurant has operated in this location, serving a variety of Mediterranean and Italian food.

S.H. KRESS BUILDING

921–923 Massachusetts Street

Constructed as two individual buildings in 1868, the two were eventually combined when S.H. Kress Company purchased both buildings. Originally owned by Frishman & Brother, the duo operated a dry goods store in 1868 here, with John Boyer's meat market moving down the street here in 1872. A variety of other businesses, including a pharmacy and a restaurant, were operated out of the buildings over the subsequent years, eventually becoming occupied by a series of grocery stores to close out the nineteenth century. Just prior to S.H. Kress's purchase of the buildings, they contained a bookstore, millinery and tailoring store, Boicourt Cycle, Home Book Company and finally the Peerless Café.

For much of the twentieth century, the building was home to the S.H. Kress department store. It operated out of the combined location from 1911 until 1965. At that time, Richard Raney, who would serve as mayor in 1967–68, bought the property to open his first Raney Drugstore, which featured a popular coffee shop. The coffee shop became a free and open space for people to congregate, discuss politics and explore social issues—for people of all races and backgrounds. It became a safe space for political conversations and local college students, as well as social and political movements, to meet and push forward their agendas. These actions resulted in the establishment of an integrated Lawrence Public Swimming Pool downtown, the Lawrence Fair Housing Ordinance and more.

A later storefront opened at 9th and Iowa and another later at 18th and Massachusetts. Raney and his father developed Hillcrest Shopping Center, where their Iowa Street store was located. Raney operated these locations, selling them nearly fifty years later to the Kroger Company in 1996. Still owned by Raney Properties, the building housed Blue Heron Furniture from 1996 to 2010, when Kansas Sampler moved in.

BLACK RECRUIT ENCAMPMENT

10th and Massachusetts Street

Located here on the morning of August 21, 1863, was a small encampment of about twenty Black recruits of the 2nd Kansas Colored Infantry. Raiders rode downtown, and upon hearing the gunfire, the soldiers immediately fled to a willow grove located about two miles downriver. There they hid with other African Americans until it was certain that the raiders had left Lawrence.

MASONIC TEMPLE

1001–1003 Massachusetts Street

Purchased on November 7, 1863, by the Methodist Church, just months following Quantrill's Raid, this site became the meeting place for the Lawrence Freemasons. Erected on July 5, 1864, this building became the town's First Methodist Church. Ownership of the building would transfer to Watkins National Bank in July 1890, but the church would continue to use the building to host its events and services.

In September 1909, the Masons purchased the lot for a standalone building. Designed by KU professor William A. Griffith in the Egyptian Revival style, construction began in 1910 and was finished in 1911. The Masons began meeting here in September while they finished the building and its furnishings that December. Once completed, it served as a meeting place for both adult and youth Masonic organizations.

Today, the building continues to showcase its unique finishes, such as its tin ceilings, wood floors and marble staircases and accents, especially at and near the grand entryway. For a number of years in the early 2000s, this building remained closed and for sale. While it continues to showcase its tin ceilings, wood floors and marble highlights, the building has since found its new long-term purpose. A nondenominational Christian church, the Greenhouse Culture, moved in in 2012, following a decade of the building sitting vacant. In early 2019, that organization moved out and across the street to 1012 Massachusetts, opening with a new café and sanctuary in the back. Once again, this historic building is looking for its newest owner.

VARSITY THEATER

1013 Massachusetts Street

Initially located here as a residential space, this building was owned by family physician John Medlicott. On April 21, 1871, it was suspected that he had poisoned and killed Isaac Miles Ruth, the business manager of the *Kansas Daily Tribune*. Medlicott was found guilty that October and sentenced to hang for his crime. However, the Kansas Supreme Court overturned the decision, and Medlicott, now a freed man, fled Kansas, ultimately ending up in Pennsylvania. It wasn't the first murder to occur in Medlicott's life. On December 15, 1870, Medlicott's wife was murdered in their home, but no one was ever tried for that crime.

The building remained a residence through the 1910s but was converted in 1914 to serve as the Varsity Theater. Featuring a pipe organ, the Varsity set itself apart from the Patee and Dickinson Theaters. The building was remodeled in 1926 with the addition of loges and a balcony to increase seating, becoming the largest theater, and said to be the most unique, in Lawrence. When a fire at the First Presbyterian Church broke out in 1929, displacing the congregation, it moved to the theater (which itself had suffered a fire in 1915) while the church was reconstructed. A renovation in 1966 included a new ceiling, an expansion of the stage area and relocation of the lobby and foyer. The theater continued to thrive here until the 1980s, passing through a series of hands until 1988, when the property was sold to United Artists, which ultimately shuttered the venue in 1997. Since that time, it received an extensive renovation to become home to the retailer Urban Outfitters.

THE GRANADA

1020 Massachusetts Street

The space that now houses the Granada Theater originally opened on Mass Street as a grocer in 1905, later serving as a skating rink, auto repair shop, a Ford and Lincoln dealership, an extensive lumberyard and, eventually, the Commonwealth Theater, owned by Stanley Earl Schwan. His remodel of the lot would become Lawrence's fourth modern-day theater, the Granada.

When the Granada was constructed originally in 1928, it was designed as a forum for vaudeville and silent movies by Boller Brothers out of Kansas City. It specialized in theater design in the Midwest during the early twentieth century. The brothers, Carl and Robert Boller, have been credited with almost one hundred theater designs that range from the smaller vaudeville venues like the Granada to the newer, grand movie palaces that started cropping up afterward. The Granada got a renovation shortly thereafter, in 1934, to convert the space into a movie theater, with Robert Montgomery's *Hide-Out* being the initial offering to audiences.

Of course, the Granada was not the only theater in town, or along Mass. Following the closure of both the Jayhawker and Patee Theaters, both

The Granada Theater, seen here in 1938, has been a Mass Street attraction for decades, offering productions from vaudeville to motion pictures to concerts. *Courtesy of the Library of Congress.*

the Granada and Varsity Theaters continued on before the rise of multi-screen venues finally put the Granada out of business in 1989. In 1999, former Douglas County District Judge Mike Ewell bought the venue and transformed it into a coffee shop and nightclub, then a comedy club and concert venue. They managed to retain much of the original structure of the building, including the ticket booth and original movie posters. Later, the venue was leased out to Mike Logan, who transformed the space into one of the premier live music venues in Lawrence, with acts as diverse as the local band The Get Up Kids to Henry Rollins, Pat Green, Marilyn Manson and Ben Folds, among others.

WATKINS COMMUNITY MUSEUM

1047 Massachusetts Street

The Watkins bank building, designed in the Richardsonian Romanesque style, was completed and opened in 1887. Since that time, it has stood as a stalwart on the northwest corner located at the southernmost intersection along Mass Street. It was designed by the Chicago architectural firm

Cobb & Ross. The red brick building's large windows, which once allowed natural light into the building, became a slight issue in the renovation and restructuring of the space for exhibitions. These pitfalls have been addressed and since have been utilized as part of the exhibition. Tall ceilings, intricate woodwork and elaborate features highlight the upper floors, led there by a double-height entry and stairway that connect the banking hall and the offices.

The bank was constructed for Jabez Bunting Watkins and his Watkins Land Mortgage Company. This would become his headquarters, having expanded his business to include real estate, titles and loans. The building's first floor was home to several offices, while the J.B. Watkins bank was located on the second floor. The third floor contained J.B.'s Mortgage Company. Following a brief setback during a nationwide economic downturn in the late 1890s, Watkins would end up owning seven corporations and more than 100,000 acres in Texas and Louisiana. His wife, Elizabeth M. "Lizzie" Watkins, would become a driving force in the philanthropy of Lawrence and at the university, pouring her efforts to scholarships at the university and the city, including the donation of the Watkins building to the city, which

Now home to the Watkins Community Museum, Jabez B. Watkins's land company and bank building, seen here around 1895, helped anchor the south end of the downtown district. *Courtesy of the Library of Congress.*

renovated it for use as its city hall and additional city offices until a new building could be constructed for such services.

The Douglas County Historical Society was established in 1933, eventually moving into Watkins's bank and operating here to this day. The museum houses exhibits and artifacts of Douglas County history, with a heavy emphasis on the history of Lawrence. Some of the most notable items on display include a printer's mallet from the *Herald of Freedom* press, pieces of the *Kansas Free State Press*'s printing press and the Mexican-American War cannon "Old Sacramento," which was used during the strife of Bleeding Kansas.

DOUGLAS COUNTY COURTHOUSE

1100 Massachusetts Street

The Douglas County Courthouse is home to multiple county departments, such as County Administration, the Commission Board, the County Clear and the Treasurer's Office, among all other county services. Douglas County was established on May 15, 1854, with county services operating out of rented

Built in 1905, the Douglas County Courthouse was designed by John G. Haskell out of Cottonwood limestone and concrete. Look around the main entrance to find a small gargoyle located on the building's clock tower. *Author's collection.*

office space since those days. Rooms here were rented whenever they were available until 1869, when Lawrence City Hall's construction was finally complete and the county ended up renting quarters within the newer building.

In 1899, Lawrence citizens voted to levy a tax to construct this courthouse. At three and a half stories and constructed out of stone, the courthouse was designed by John G. Haskell and completed in 1905. Designed in the Richardsonian Romanesque style, it was constructed out of rough-hewn Cottonwood limestone and concrete. The raised basement is evident from the outside, and the building's apex features a six-story tall clock tower, while inside is a central lobby with a round opening leading to a glass dome. Two major entrances are located on the west and north sides. Looking up at the west side's main entrance, look for a small gargoyle on the clock tower, just above the first floor. The courthouse has recently undergone a major renovation.

J.E. STUBBS BUILDING

1101–1103 Massachusetts Street

The Stubbs building is the site of a former early twentieth-century drugstore and soda counter called the Corner Drug Store, primarily because the site locates its main entrance on the corner. Constructed in the Classical Revival style in 1909 by J.E. Stubbs, one of the People State Bank's directors, which had been chartered in 1905, the building sits opposite the Douglas County Courthouse, on the south end of the Central Business District along Mass Street. By 1918, the space contained a drugstore, along with a popular soda counter. The building's main entrance sat on the street corner and contained commercial space in its northwest corner, which housed a manicuring salon. The south half of the building sat vacant.

For decades, the building served Lawrence as the Corner Drug Store; a cheese and deli shop operated out of a rear entry. When a new group purchased the building, it needed extensive repairs throughout. The multi-year renovation project was finished in 2019, respecting the original framework while also restoring other exterior finishes that had been removed in the past. Today, the longtime ice cream parlor Sylas & Maddy's occupies the ground-floor space, while children's shelter nonprofit Shelter Inc. has moved into the space previously occupied by the cheese store.

SOUTH PARK

1141 Massachusetts Street

South Park was a part of the original 1854 townsite for Kansas. Originally, the site was a large meadow, used as a public area for community members to grow crops and graze livestock. Currently, South Park covers fourteen acres of Lawrence's original townsite in downtown Lawrence. In the town's original plat, South Park covered eight city blocks, then evenly divided into four separate parks: Lafayette, Hamilton, Washington and Franklin Parks. As the town grew and adapted the layout, the parkland changed but has retained much of its original landscape. The park played an important role during Quantrill's Raid on August 21, 1863, serving as an ad hoc staging area during the event.

Once the town began to rebuild, Lawrence used South Park as a central focal point for the community. The William Kelly Bandstand, better known as the South Park Gazebo, was erected in May 1906 and continues to be used today, especially during the summer band series. Also located in the park is the Roosevelt Fountain, moved here in the 1980s; it was dedicated on August 31, 1910, with President Theodore Roosevelt in attendance.

Also located in the park is the 1963 South Park Recreation Center, which now houses the Parks & Recreation Administrative Offices, as well as additional event space. To this day, South Park has served as a hub for families and includes playground equipment, a wading pool, large open areas for a variety of activities and a butterfly garden, which was constructed in conjunction with the University of Kansas's famed Monarch Watch.

ENGLISH LUTHERAN CHURCH

1040 New Hampshire Street

When it was constructed around 1870, the English Lutheran Church was a two-story rusticated limestone church constructed atop a limestone block foundation. Next door to the old church building is the Lutheran church's original parsonage. Built in the Gothic Revival style by pioneer Kansas architect John G. Haskell, this structure was expanded for a growing congregation in 1900. At one point, this church building was slated for

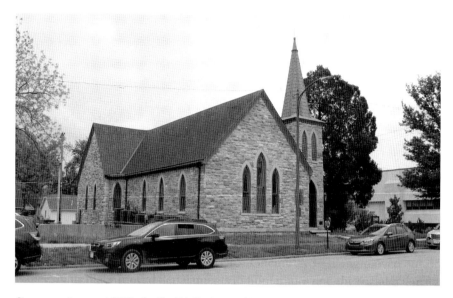

Constructed around 1870, the English Lutheran Church was constructed by famed Kansas architect John G. Haskell. It has since been adapted for use as office space. *Author's collection.*

demolition. Following a four-year legal dispute, the building ended up being sold, restored and adapted for reuse as a modern office space. On November 6, 1993, Kansas Governor Joan Finney reopened the building.

TRAMPLED RECRUITS

933 New Hampshire Street

A marker denotes another spot for a small encampment on the morning of August 21, 1863. These were white volunteers, many only teenagers. A group of raiders on horseback found and trampled the tents, killing seventeen of the twenty-one unarmed, and unprepared, recruits. The only arms the recruits had been supplied with were old, worthless muskets affixed with bayonets. They would only have been good to stand guard, not to fight with. Cosma T. Colman, a raid survivor, managed to run across an open lot to Joe Rawlin's back fence with another recruit named Charley. As they ran, they saw the raiders ahead of them on Rhode Island Street. Colman managed to clear the fence, but as he turned to help his fellow recruit, he watched Charley get shot in the back by the raiders.

DONNELLY BROTHERS LIVERY STABLE

700 New Hampshire Street

James Donnelly and his siblings Neil and John arrived in Lawrence in 1857. James and Neil managed a livery stable here, where they tended to both horses and vehicles, starting in 1873. Additionally, they rented out space here to pay. It garnered a reputation throughout the state and was a favorite with the KU students. James ran the livery stable business for several years, while Neil lived in Kansas City, which is where John relocated and remained, operating a mercantile business until his death in 1892.

In April 1897, a fire broke out, consuming the barn, nineteen horses and numerous vehicles. They continued their business in a rear shed that survived the flames before constructing a large brick building, which opened in August of that year. The barn would become home to nearly one hundred horses, half owned by them and the other half belonging to boarders. Additionally, they could house 125 vehicles, about 40 owned by them and the rest by private individuals. The brothers employed fourteen men, managed by James. Eventually, the business ran its course, and the building housed

James and Neil Donnelly operated their popular livery stable here starting in 1873, eventually converting it to house mechanized vehicles as well. It was well known throughout the state and became a favorite with students at KU. *Author's collection.*

a variety of tenants, with Borders Bookstore arriving in the late 1990s. Borders sought to demolish the livery stable structure but folded to public outcry and left two of the walls standing as part of its new building. Since Borders' evacuation of the building in 2011 due to impending bankruptcy, several proposals for the newer building have been made, with none moving forward. You can still see the stalls, since they are bricked over, along the New Hampshire Street frontage wall.

LAWRENCE POST OFFICE BUILDING

645 New Hampshire Street

This building, constructed in 1906, was designed in the Beaux-Arts style for use as Lawrence's primary post office. It became Lawrence's first federal building and replaced the previous locations of the itinerant post office, which landed at the Bowersock Opera House in 1870. An addition to the post office came in 1930 that doubled the space. The masonry and steel frame structure was rehabbed in 2001–02 to become office space for the *Journal-World* newspaper. The project uncovered skylights and other windows that had been painted over, included the retention of the terrazzo floor and marble inlay, and matching glass globes for the chandeliers were installed. The post office closed in 1973 and was purchased by the university to be used for storage before the Simons family bought it for use as their newspaper facilities.

The *Journal-World* title didn't come into existence until 1911, but in some form it has existed since 1858. W.C. Simons served as the paper's editor from 1891 until his death in 1952, handing the paper to his son, Dolph Simons Sr., who would later pass the paper to his son, Dolph Jr. Many changes in the early 2000s came to the media empire created by the Simons family before they ultimately sold the newspaper in 2016 to the West Virginia company Odgen Newspapers, ending the family's 125-year ownership. In 2019, operations moved to an office in North Lawrence, and the old post office building is now occupied by Blue Cross Blue Shield of Kansas.

In 2019, the new owner, Ogden Newspapers, another long-running family-owned company, moved the newspaper's offices from the historic post office building to an office in North Lawrence. The building retains much of its historical integrity. Not far from this location, now covered up by the

From 1906 until 1973, this building served as Lawrence's primary post office. For the better part of the early twenty-first century, the retrofitted building was home to the *Lawrence Journal-World* newspaper. *Author's collection.*

newspaper's former press facility, was once the site of the first home built in Lawrence. It was a simple log cabin belonging to Clark Steans and was located at what would now be 620 Massachusetts Street.

REUTER ORGAN COMPANY

612 New Hampshire Street

Since the late nineteenth century, this building has seen Lawrence's industrial operations change. The first at this location was constructed in 1882 and became home to the Wilder Brothers Shirt Factory until 1917. J. Frank and Charles E. Wilder specialized in made-to-order shirts, along with men's undergarments, and provided laundry services. The brothers' business thrived, and they constructed this building to house operations in 1882. Initially, the building stood three stories high and used water power generated by Bowersock Dam to operate the sewing machines. The company peaked between 1890 and 1910, producing twenty thousand

This site was originally home to the Wilder Brothers Shirt Factory, which closed in 1916, and then the Reuter Organ Company moved in during 1919. It used the property, expanding and improving the site, until it closed in 2001. Despite years of neglect, it is seeing new life breathed into it. *Author's collection.*

shirts annually and adding a fourth story to the building. The factory ended up shutting its doors in 1916, ultimately being purchased by the Reuter Organ Company in 1919.

Reuter Organ Company set up shop in Lawrence for nearly a century. Purchasing the building in 1919, it used the property as its headquarters until 2001, adding the additional brick building next door in 1927. The location was beneficial, as the building's proximity to the river and the dam meant access to water power and easy shipments via nearby rail lines. The company renovated the stone building once it moved in, constructing additions to make its organ assembly operation easier and to include a lumber kiln. The Great Depression and World War II had a severe impact on the company, and near the war's end, the organ company had to close shops, just before being awarded a contract to build shipping boxes for munitions. Business picked up again following the war, and by 1948, Reuters was the only organ company between St. Louis and California. As time wore on, though, the demand for organs declined, and the company slowly ceased operations. After twenty years of neglect, the Wilder Building was in danger of collapse. A new roof and supports were added through a major rehabilitation project. Today, the properties are being converted for modern office and residential space.

FIRST UNITED METHODIST CHURCH SITE

724 Vermont Street

On a wall adjacent to the bus stop at 7th Street and Vermont, there is a small bronze plaque that locates the original site of the First United Methodist Church. The church was organized by two circuit-riding Methodist ministers shortly after the founding of the town. Following Quantrill's August 1863 raid, the church doubled as both a morgue and a triage camp, being one of the few structures left unscathed. The original church structure lasted until the 1940s, serving a variety of other congregations before being transformed into a residence. The congregation itself had moved to a new brick church in 1865 and then to its present location, a stone Richardsonian Romanesque building designed by John Haskell and located at 946 Vermont Street in 1891.

LUCY HOBBS TAYLOR BUILDING

809 Vermont Street

The Lucy Hobbs Taylor Building, constructed in 1871, and its neighbor to the south are the only buildings still standing that are original to downtown's Vermont Street. Built to serve as a combined residence and office, it has been in use continuously for both purposes ever since. The original owners were James and Lucy Hobbs Taylor, the first woman to earn a Doctor of Dental Surgery degree. She and her husband both practiced dentistry and eventually ran a large and successful practice here for twenty-six years. Following James's death in 1886, she closed the practice and got involved in politics and women's rights until her death in 1910. Her influence in the field of dentistry opened many doors for women in the medical field.

While the exterior of the home's brick Italianate structure has changed very little, its interior has been modified multiple times during its existence. It was used primarily as a residence between an auction sale in 1916 and 1939, when veterinarian T.J. Leasure remodeled the interior to use as an animal hospital. Most of the alterations came inside on the first floor, but he also replaced a south bay window with glass blocks and painted the exterior bricks white. When Leasure sold the building in 1969, another vet continued to use it as a hospital for the next few years, removing the front porch and enclosing the side one. Paula Oldehoeft purchased the building in 1979 to use as a hair salon. That same year, rehabilitation work started on the Taylor Building, recovering some of the original interior and exterior features.

CARNEGIE CITY LIBRARY

200 9th Street

Constructed in 1904, Lawrence's Carnegie Library is an excellent extant example of Neoclassical architecture. The library building was designed in the Beaux-Arts style by architect George A. Belinghof, while a rear addition came to the building in 1937 as a part of the Works Progress Administration and was constructed, in part, to accommodate the library's growing collection of books and materials. The library was in operation until 1972, when a new building was constructed a few blocks north. The library would serve as the Lawrence Arts Center until 2002, before reopening in a new space in 2011.

Lawrence's early city library building was one of Andrew Carnegie's vast system of libraries that he funded. It was constructed in 1904 and operated here until a new building opened in 1972. *Author's collection.*

Today, the building serves as the headquarters and visitors center to the National Park Service's Freedom's Frontier National Historic Area. The location sits central in Lawrence's historic environs for the struggle over slavery and freedom. Additionally, the site itself holds historic importance to that narrative. Located just outside the entrance, affixed to the building's wall, there is a small plaque that commemorates poet Langston Hughes, who was raised by his maternal grandmother in Lawrence and was a frequent visitor to the library.

PLYMOUTH CONGREGATIONAL CHURCH

925 Vermont Street

Plymouth Congregational Church, an affiliate of the United Church of Christ, was established just months following the opening of the Kansas Territory in 1854. The congregation's first sermon, given by Reverend Samuel Y. Lum, was held on October 1, 1854, in a mudbrick boardinghouse.

Plymouth Congregational Church, seen here in 1856, was established months prior to the opening of settlement in Kansas Territory in 1854. This building replaced the original mudbrick boardinghouse. *Courtesy of the Library of Congress.*

Three years later, Reverend Richard Cordley became the pastor, and the congregation moved into its first permanent building, the "Stone Church," which would remain under construction until 1862. Cordley was an abolitionist who supported the Free State movement, and several members of his congregation were killed by the raiders in 1863. His own home was burned in the raid, but the church managed to survive unscathed. His subsequent book on the raid, an early history of Lawrence, has proved invaluable to researchers.

As Lawrence rebuilt and grew, it was evident that a larger church was needed to serve the congregation. The present-day church building, built in 1870 and designed by John G. Haskell, is listed in the National Register of Historic Places. It is known as the "Brick Church," and Haskell finished the Victorian-era church, featuring Gothic and Romanesque Revival characteristics, in May 1870 and included windows created in England. The parish house was added in 1916, although it was damaged by fire in 1955. Additional renovation work, which included the expansion and rebuilding of sections of the church, took place following a fire. Additional renovations came to various parts of the church twice, once in 1992 and again in 2001.

TRINITY EPISCOPAL CHURCH

1011 Vermont Street

Trinity Parish was one of the early churches in town, established in 1857. The parish's original church was consecrated on this site in July 1859. Samuel Reynolds had recognized the need for an Episcopal church in town. In response, Amos A. Lawrence fulfilled his wish. Out of this original church was created the University of Kansas through the efforts of Reverend Robert Oliver. In 1865, Reverend Oliver became the first chancellor of KU, helping lead the effort to build North College Hall, opening on September 16, 1866.

Trinity Church continued to expand and, as such, needed a larger building. This new church building opened on Easter in 1873. The original building continued to be used, serving as both chapel and a parish hall. In April 1955, Trinity was completely gutted by fire. Its walnut interior and nearly all its stained-glass windows were destroyed in the flames. Less than a year later, in March 1956, the rebuilt structure was rededicated. In the

Trinity Episcopal Church was one of the earliest churches in Lawrence. The University of Kansas got its launch through the efforts of Reverend Robert Oliver. In 1865, he became KU's first chancellor. *Author's collection.*

early 1970s, the original 1959 church building was razed to make room for classrooms, offices and a new parish hall. In the late 1980s, the continually growing congregation called for more space. Trinity helped establish the second Episcopal parish in town, St. Margaret's Episcopal Church, which is in far western Lawrence on West 6th Street.

LAWRENCE COMMUNITY BUILDING

115 West 11th Street

Originally designed as an armory for the city in 1940, this structure was replaced in the 1950s with a new armory located north of 6th Street. The armory was established in 1863 to contain the muskets provided by the State of Kansas and also held all the firearms owned by individual citizens. This localized concentration of arms likely helped Quantrill's guerrillas in their raid of the town in August 1863, as citizens had no time to make it to the armory. In fact, most of the armory's guns were left in the armory by the raiders. In 1864, blockhouses were built to allow the local militia to defend Lawrence, and by that time, the use of the armory had come to an end.

The Lawrence Community Building has become a central gathering place for a bevy of recreational activities and, like all City of Lawrence Recreation Centers, is free to Douglas County residents. Today, the facility hosts locker and shower facilities, a full-size gymnasium, a weight and exercise room, a dance studio and multiple meeting and activity rooms.

HASKELL UNIVERSITY

Founded in 1884 as a residential boarding school for Native American children, Haskell University opened as the United States Indian Industrial Training School. It was originally established to assimilate tribal children into mainstream America through its educational offerings, and the first twenty-two students enrolled in grades one through five. At the school, the students would receive training in both agricultural and vocational trades—boys learning trades such as shoemaking, blacksmithing and farming, while girls studied homemaking skills such as cooking and sewing. The school's name was changed to Haskell Institute in 1887, and it expanded its offerings beyond elementary grades in 1894. The school had shifted its focus away from assimilation by the turn of the century, and by 1927, it was offering post-secondary courses. In 1970, it transitioned to Haskell Indian Junior College, and in 1993, it changed to Haskell Indian Nations University. Operated by the U.S. Bureau of Indian Affairs and offering both associate and baccalaureate degrees, Haskell is a leading institute of higher education for American Indians and Alaskan Natives.

Haskell University star athletes A. Carpenter, J. Levi and George Levi are seen outside the White House in 1923. *Courtesy of the Library of Congress.*

CULTURAL CENTER AND MUSEUM

2411 Barker Avenue

Haskell's Cultural Center and Museum was opened in September 2002 to serve as a steward of tribal materials, traditions and cultural arts. The exhibits here convey the story of Haskell's evolution from a government boarding school focusing on assimilation to a present-day accredited university. Open weekdays only, the museum is free (of course, donations are accepted). The museum houses roughly two thousand cultural items, a collection of historic photographs and numerous archival documents and reports spanning the history of Haskell. It covers the story of everyday life for the students, their social lives and their education. Throughout the museum are exhibitions that celebrate tribal military history, including the life and accomplishments of Chester Nez, a Navajo code talker who was an alum of KU. The museum also manages the Healing Garden, restored by the Haskell Greenhouse, where specific tribal herbs are maintained.

HASKELL MEMORIAL STADIUM

400 Indian Avenue

The Haskell football stadium and archway were constructed largely by the Haskell student body. Native American donors from throughout the country gave to the project, which was dedicated in 1926. Viewed with great pride by Native Americans throughout the country, its size and grandeur represented the prominence of Haskell and several other Native American schools during the 1920s. Throughout the early 1900s, Haskell's football team was one of the best in the nation. Athletes such as John Levi, Jim Thorpe and Billy Mills all played on this field. The new stadium could host more than ten thousand attendees.

A celebration was held from October 27 to October 30, 1926. Both Jim Thorpe and John Levi participated, with Thorpe kicking balls and Levi throwing passes. There was a powwow, a buffalo feast and a "Hiawatha" performance by Haskell students. The celebration concluded with a football game against Pennsylvania's Bucknell University, with Haskell winning 36–0. Along the way, before and after the new stadium was built,

The Haskell Archway, along with the football stadium, was constructed primarily by Haskell students in 1926. The school's football team and other sports figures were some of the best in the country during the early twentieth century. *Author's collection.*

Haskell's team defeated the likes of KU, Mizzou and Nebraska and would play against Notre Dame, Wisconsin, Texas and LSU. The apex came when they beat the national powerhouse team from Baylor. Unfortunately, a lack of funding caused the university to discontinue the football program in the 1930s. While it was later revived, it never quite met the fanfare of the past. Today, HINU competes against area junior colleges.

COFFIN SPORTS COMPLEX

515 Indian Avenue

Built in 1981, the Coffin Sports Complex once was the site of two other historic buildings on the HINU campus. The Tahoma hospital building once sat on the present site of the sports complex. The forty-two-bed hospital was constructed in 1906 and razed in 1980. Additionally, located south of the building was a building for teachers' quarters, built in 1916.

Located inside the Coffin Sports Complex is an Olympic-size swimming pool, racquetball courts and basketball courts. It also is currently home to the American Indian Athletic Hall of Fame. It was named for Troy Coffin of the Prairie Band Potawatomi. In 1945, Coffin was Haskell's head football coach and later its athletic director. Coffin's son, Doug, designed the Medicine Wheel Totem Pole, which is displayed in front of the Coffin Complex.

AMERICAN INDIAN ATHLETIC HALL OF FAME

515 Indian Avenue

Located on the Haskell campus, the American Indian Athletic Hall of Fame was built to recognize athletes of American Indian heritage and to serve as a model for Native youth to strive for their own excellence. The hall was founded in 1972 by Robert L. Bennett of the Oneida tribe and Louis R. Bruce of the Mohawk and Sioux. Both men were former commissioners of Indian Affairs in Washington, D.C. Olympic gold medal winner Billy Mills was appointed its first coordinator. Highlighted here are the achievements of Jim Thorpe, Billy Mills, Sonny Sixkiller, John Levi, Moses Yellow Horse and ninety other athletes. For thirty-four years, the American Indian Hall of Fame was housed in the student union and girls' gym and presently resides inside Haskell's boys' gymnasium.

HASKELL CEMETERY

650 Kiowa Avenue

This small cemetery is located on the edge of campus. The earliest known burial here came in 1885, and the grounds were used for more than a half century, with the last burial coming in 1943. About one hundred Haskell students are buried here. Engraved on the markers are the child's name, tribal affiliation and dates of birth and death. Additionally, on some of the markers you can find the cause of death, such as tuberculosis, pneumonia and accidental death. The cemetery is fenced off for safety and protective purposes. If you find yourself inside, please be respectful of the offerings left behind.

TECUMSEH HALL

2445 Choctaw Avenue

Tecumseh Hall is named for the Shawnee chief and was built in 1915. It was constructed to serve as the boys' gymnasium. Today, the first floor has a basketball court and is used for additional campus activities and events. Additionally, the *Indian Leader* student newspaper and the student activity offices are located here.

THE HASKELL BANDSTAND

2445 Choctaw Avenue

Now called the Gazebo, the Haskell Bandstand was built in 1908 following the destruction of the previous one in a windstorm. It was located between old Winona and Osceola Halls, about 220 feet from present-day Tecumseh Hall. Music was a consistently enjoyed student activity on the Haskell campus, and the bandstand was a favorite place to be. It was used frequently for concerts. The Haskell band was renowned and played at events throughout the country, including a gig at the 1904 World's Fair in St. Louis.

HIAWATHA HALL

2435 Choctaw Avenue

Dedicated in 1899, Hiawatha Hall is the oldest structure on Haskell's campus. It was named after the Onondaga leader who helped create the Iroquois League. As the college was established as a boarding school for Native American children, it reflected the U.S. government's goal of eradicating the cultural, communal and religious ways of Native

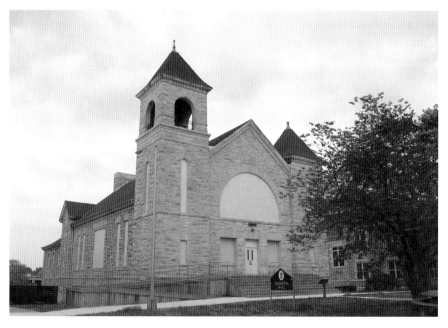

Hiawatha Hall is the oldest structure on the campus of Haskell Indian Nations University and named for the Onondaga leader. It is listed as a National Historic Landmark. *Author's collection*.

American tribes through assimilation. The United Methodist Church provided funding for the construction of Hiawatha Hall to perpetuate that cause, as this limestone building was to serve as a campus chapel. For more than a century, it served as an auditorium; however, it eventually suffered neglect and has been closed to the public since 2005. Since it was listed as a National Historic Landmark, a multimillion-dollar restoration project has been started to help restore this and other campus buildings. Crews placed a new roof on Hiawatha in 2017.

UNIVERSITY OF KANSAS

Founded in Lawrence, Kansas, on September 12, 1866, the University of Kansas started as a preparatory school with fifty-five students. Efforts to establish the school dated to 1855, and it earned its charter as Lawrence University but was slowed due to the Civil War. With forty acres of land from Charles Robinson and his wife, Sara Tappan Robinson, $10,000 for an endowment from Amos Lawrence and another $5,000 from the citizens of Lawrence, the university had its location and funding. The site selected was Mount Oread, then called Hogback Ridge.

The school's Board of Regents held its first meeting in March 1865, giving the university its official founding date. Work on the first college building, now referred to as Old North College, began later that year. Preparatory classes began on September 12, 1866, with college-level classes beginning in 1869. The first class graduated in 1873, consisting of four students. The first degree was a Doctor of Divinity, awarded to the abolitionist preacher Richard Cordley. Since that time, the university has expanded beyond a few buildings and now encompasses the better part of central Lawrence, along with KU Edwards Campus in Overland Park, Kansas, and additional satellite campuses in Leavenworth, Wichita, Salina and Kansas City. Since its founding, there have been eighteen chancellors, along with one interim chancellor for the state's flagship educational institution. Today, KU hosts fourteen academic schools, offering more than four hundred degree and certificate programs.

Taken by Alexander Gardner in 1867, this shot of the Old North College building overlooking Lawrence and the Kansas River was taken atop Mount Oread one year after classes began at the new University of Kansas. *Courtesy of the Boston Public Library.*

ECUMENICAL CHRISTIAN MINISTRIES

1204 Oread Avenue

Historically, this building is "part of KU but not of KU," sitting just on the edge of campus atop Mount Oread. The United Presbyterian Church, also known as the Ecumenical Christian Ministries Building, provides people meeting space inside a place of autonomy. Constructed out of concrete, brick, steel and glass, this Modern Movement–style building was constructed in 1959–60. At the time of construction, this area along Oread Avenue was dotted with both residences and commercial buildings, such as the Gaslight Tavern and the Rock Chalk Café.

A campus ministry was initiated by the Presbyterian Church in a home on Tennessee Street in 1905 (since demolished). In 1910, it constructed Westminster Hall (also demolished) at 1221 Oread, one block south of the current building. This new larger building replaced Westminster. Initially, it served as a campus ministry building to serve Christians and those of other faiths, while also providing space for a variety of student and community groups advocating peace and justice during the 1960s and 1970s. It grew as

Sitting just outside the KU campus, the Ecumenical Christian Ministries building has been a place of worship and a meeting place for those searching for autonomy while advocating peace and justice. *Author's collection.*

a place to meet and mobilize over sensitive issues at the time. It continues to serve this function to this day.

One of the many highlights inside includes the second-story chapel, which holds up to 250 people. The natural light here is brought in through four panels of windows on the north and south sides, the north of which offers a view of the Wakarusa Valley, while the south looks toward the KU campus.

BRICK'S CAFÉ SIT-INS

1231 Oread Avenue

Currently the site of a parking garage for the north end of campus, this space once was the site of Brick's Café. During the late afternoon of April 15, 1948, students from the KU chapter of the Committee on Racial Equality (CORE) held a sit-in here, which like many Lawrence establishments refused to serve African Americans. The students chose Brick's primarily because of its proximity to campus but also because it was well known that it depended on the business of students, a group that was often more open to racial integration. Protesting students began to filter in around 4:00 p.m., first white students and then mixed-race groups, sitting in booths and distributing handbills about their protest.

The owner, Mr. Murphy, refused to negotiate and would not serve the students. By 6:00 p.m., about fifteen to twenty white males had arrived inside to provide Murphy with assistance. At around 7:15 p.m., they approached an African American man seated in the back booth and informed him that he was trespassing and needed to leave. When he refused, he was dragged out and onto the floor. Regardless, he sat back down in the booth peacefully. The police arrived at this point and decided that they were fine with CORE members being thrown out. With that, they proceeded to physically carry the protestors outside. The nonviolent nature of CORE members is probably what kept the situation from escalating any further. While their efforts did not end segregation, it established a trend that was followed by more demonstrations, petitions and other sit-ins.

JAYHAWK WELCOME CENTER

1266 Oread Avenue

The University of Kansas's new visitor center, covering thirty thousand square feet, opened in 2023 and sits adjacent to the newly renovated Adams Alumni Center. The university brought its primary point for visitors closer to the main entrance of campus, rather than its previous location off Iowa Street, near the Daisy Hill dormitories. In addition to being the home to the Office of Admissions, the space includes meeting rooms, a large video screen, digital displays and a photo booth. Many of these technological opportunities provide visitors with alumni success stories, notable Jayhawks, KU traditions and the university's vast history of discoveries, research and innovations. This is a great place for those wanting to visit the university and get a quick overview of student life and its history.

SMITH HALL

1300 Oread Avenue

Smith Hall was dedicated in October 1967; however, the land that holds the buildings occupying this space did not become university property until

1998. The location was formerly Myers Hall, a privately owned building owned by and housing the Kansas Bible Chair, an entity outside of KU. It taught courses on Christianity and religious history. Chancellor Strong felt that groups and the university's approaches were very similar, so the university began soliciting private donations for the creation of Myers Hall, which was completed in 1906.

By the 1960s, a new facility was needed. The Bible Chair and other private groups began fundraising for a new building, which would become Smith Hall, named after Irma Smith, the project's largest donor. It was designed in the mid-century modern style, and architect Charles Marshall included two prominent pieces of art that are still highlights near the entrance to campus. Here you will find a statue of Moses, designed by KU professor and sculptor Elden Tefft, kneeling and

Home to KU's Religious Studies department, Smith Hall is easily recognizable with its statue of Moses kneeling and praying in front of the "Burning Bush" stained-glass window. *Author's collection.*

praying in front of Marshall's stained-glass window, "Burning Bush." The building itself houses the university's Religious Studies Department, the William J. Moore Library, classrooms and faculty offices. In 2023, it was one of a few buildings on a "mission critical" list to be demolished. Facing public backlash, Chancellor Douglas Girod placed the decision to demolish on hold—until the decisions of a future campus master plan.

KANSAS MEMORIAL UNION

1301 Jayhawk Boulevard

The idea for a student union came about in the 1910s, as the growing student body was increasingly demanding it. It was funded by the "Million

Located inside the Memorial Union, the university radio station, KJHK 90.7 FM, has been the voice of Lawrence's independent radio since 1975. *Author's collection.*

Dollar Drive," which began in 1920, as the university began to fund memorials to the 127 men and 2 women from KU who died during the First World War in the form of a new football stadium and a student union. By late 1921, the first sections of McCook Field had been completed. The hillside site for the union building to its southeast was selected so the two would be visible to each other. The original brick and limestone student union was designed by the Chicago firm of Pond & Pond, with the cornerstone being laid in April 1930. The original memorial union building stood at only 80 by 135 feet when it officially opened in September 1927. Over the next decade, lounges, game rooms, a ballroom and a cafeteria were completed, and construction finally ended in 1938. Major additions came in 1952, 1961 and the late 1980s. A massive fire set on April 20, 1970, via arson, gutted the union's upper two floors, and the repairs took nearly a year to complete.

Today, the Memorial Union is now joined with the Burge Union and the DeBruce Center as campus unions. Located here, however, is a bevy of services and a great historic overview of the KU campus. Meeting and reception rooms are joined by lounges, a food court, a gallery, convenience shops, offices, service organizations, KJHK (the student radio station), KU Bookstore, a print shop, gift shops, multiple study areas, auditoriums and more. Throughout the building, there are numerous historic items on display along with interpretive panels. This includes the story of the "Rock Chalk, Jayhawk" chant, artifacts from Old Fraser Hall, various displays of Jayhawks throughout history and displays honoring those fallen soldiers in whose memory the building was constructed. One soldier of note is KU graduate William T. Fitzsimons. He was the first American to die during World War I; he had previously worked with Lewis Lindsay Dyche to craft the "Panorama" exhibit. He was killed in a 1917 German air attack at the French Field Hospital.

SPOONER HALL

1340 Jayhawk Boulevard

While KU had a library from its inception, that collection was held in Old North College, the original university building. As the campus expanded, the library collection was moved. Eventually, it became evident that the university needed a standalone library building. William Spooner, who wanted to construct the library as well as a new chancellor's home for his nephew, Francis Snow, donated the money. Construction began in 1893 on Spooner Hall, designed by Henry Van Brunt in the Romanesque Revival style, and was finished by 1894. Looking at the apex of the peak on the front of the building, one will see a gazing owl, a symbol of knowledge. Follow its stare across the street to Dyche Hall, the home of the Natural History Museum, and you will find another owl, staring back. When these

Spooner Hall, KU's original library building, was completed in 1894, the year this photograph was taken. It has served as museums for art and anthropology and is primarily used for interdisciplinary events. *Courtesy of the Library of Congress.*

two buildings were finished, they were located at the primary entrance to campus. The two owls served as a virtual "barrier" that students crossed as they headed onto campus.

The library collection quickly outgrew its home and, by 1920, had become too large for the space. A new library plan was developed, and in 1924, Watson Library was constructed. Two years after, Spooner Hall was converted into the Spooner-Thayer Museum of Art, housing the newly acquired collection of Sallie Casey Thayer. In 1978, this was also moved out when the university constructed the Spencer Art Museum behind Memorial Union. From 1972 to 2002, the building served as the Museum of Anthropology. Today, the building serves primarily as the Commons, a university event space that looks to bridge the gap between the disciplines on campus, melding science and art, journalism and prose, hosting speaking engagements and housing special exhibitions and events.

DYCHE HALL

1345 Jayhawk Boulevard

Among many outstanding buildings on campus, Dyche Hall stands out from the rest by a clear shot. As part of the entryway to campus at the turn of the twentieth century, Dyche was in partnership with its neighbor across the street, Spooner Hall, the campus library, serving as a portal of knowledge. It was designed in 1901–02 by Kansas City architects Walter C. Root and George W. Siemens in a Venetian Romanesque style. Made of Oread limestone, the building features an arched doorway for the main entrance and a steepled tower. Exploration of the exterior of the building reveals elaborate stone ornamentations of creatures, real and imagined (including what may be the first representation of the Jayhawk); plants; prominent scientist's names; and multiple grotesques, some holding shields denoting the "Rock Chalk, Jayhawk."

It was named for Professor Lewis Lindsay Dyche following his death; it was his work that made the construction of this building possible. A world-famous explorer and collector of specimens from every corner of the world, Dyche had begun teaching while a KU undergraduate and became the school's chair of the zoology and taxidermy departments and curator of birds and mammals. His mounting of the "Panorama of North

There is so much to explore on the exterior of Dyche Hall that it is almost impossible to list all its features. You can find fossils, elaborate stone ornamentations of real and imaginary creatures, names of scientists and multiple grotesques. Inside there are more than 350 exhibits and storage for millions of scientific specimens. *Author's collection.*

American Animals and Plants" for the 1893 World's Columbian Exposition in Chicago made the Kansas Pavilion, and the university, the talk of the fair. Chancellor Snow, as a result, pounced to capitalize on the success and lobbied successfully for a new building. It opened in October 1902 and was completed the following year. It featured the "Panorama" exhibit from the fair and his 1891 taxidermy work on the horse Comanche, long believed to be the only survivor of the U.S. Cavalry force on the Custer battlefield of Little Bighorn in June 1876. More than 350 exhibits are featured inside, including everything from dinosaurs (look up just inside the entrance to see a massive Mosasaur) to viruses and topics from colony collapse to evolution. Classrooms and specimens in storage also abound inside. A 1930s renovation project, which closed the museum due to safety issues for nearly a decade, allowed the building to be improved. An addition in 1963 doubled the complex in size, and another addition in 1995 created space for millions of specimens stored in alcohol.

DANFORTH CHAPEL

1405 Jayhawk Boulevard

Constructed at the tail end of World War II, Danforth Chapel is KU's nondenominational campus. German prisoners of war from Camp Lawrence (located near Haskell and East 11th Street) constructed the chapel building. Fifteen German prisoners were detailed to work on campus, specifically on the chapel and its grounds. The chapel was designed by KU graduate Edward Tanner, who in lieu of payment asked that the building's design be dedicated in honor of his mother, Harriet A. Tanner. Dedicated on April 2, 1946, Danforth Chapel quickly became a hot spot as a wedding venue. Two months following its opening on June 17, 1946, seven Jayhawk couples were married. One young couple, however, were able to use the space earlier. On March 20, 1946, the couple was married, nearly two weeks prior to the dedication.

The plans for the chapel came about during a September 1944 meeting between Chancellor Deane Malott and William Danforth, benefactor and a founder of Ralston Purina. Danforth liked the design offered by Edward Tanner's proposal and provided additional funding, with the rest of the funding being secured by the university. Since that time, Danforth has shifted its Christian origin into an interfaith space. It has become one of the most iconic campus landmarks, located near the university's historic campus entrance.

LIPPINCOTT HALL

1410 Jayhawk Boulevard

Originally, this building served the campus as Green Hall. The only evidence of that remaining is the statue located on the sidewalk out front that adorns the building. There you see a statue of inaugural law school Dean James Woods Green standing with a student. It was constructed in 1904 and dedicated in November 1905 to house the university's law school, which at that time was using several buildings and was seeing increasing enrollment. The statue was dedicated on June 9, 1924; he had served KU from 1978 until his November 1919 death. Daniel Chester French, the sculptor of the famous Abraham Lincoln statue in Washington, D.C., was eventually chosen and modeled the student on Alfred C. Alford, the first KU graduate killed during the Spanish-American War.

The building was rechristened in 1977 as Lippincott Hall. Green Hall had recently moved to its own newer building, the law school having moved frequently over the years. Under Dean Green, the school had bounced from Old Fraser Hall and Blake Hall. In 1904, the regents provided construction money for a new law school, petitioned for by students and named Green Hall. Rather than being torn down, Lippincott remains and today is listed in the National Register of Historic Places and houses the Wilcox Classics Museum.

FRASER HALL

1415 Jayhawk Boulevard

Constructed of cottonwood and limestone, Fraser Hall opened in March 1967. Visible for miles around, the imposing structure sits on the second-highest point on Mount Oread. Designed by State Architect James Canole and T.R. Griest, this iteration of Fraser Hall is more than twice the size of its predecessor, also named Fraser Hall. It houses several of the social sciences

The university's original Fraser Hall, seen here around 1873, was a massive landmark atop Mount Oread. It, like its successor, could be seen for miles in the distance. *Courtesy of DeGolyer Library, Southern Methodist University.*

departments, such as anthropology, sociology and psychology, among other classrooms, offices and clinics.

The original Fraser Hall, designed by John G. Haskell, was located only fifty feet west of the present building. On a very dry day, you might be able to find remnants of the old foundation, peeking up through short grass. Built in 1872 and originally named University Building in 1877, it was renamed after KU's second chancellor, John Fraser, in 1897. When they designed the new building, they retained the design of the old towers, which highlights the university's viewscape from afar. After the original's razing for the new building, architectural details were salvaged and can now be found across campus in places like the Kansas Union, the Adams Alumni Center and other campus structures.

THE OUTLOOK

1532 Lilac Lane

This home, set back from the street, is the private residence of the University of Kansas's chancellor. One still can get a good view of the home from the surrounding street and campus. It was constructed in 1912 to be the home of banker Jabez B. Watkins and his wife, Elizabeth. Following Jabez's death, Elizabeth became very involved in the community of both the city and the university. Her first donation to KU was for the funding of a scholarship hall for women students, now known as Watkins Hall. Another donation followed a decade later for Watkins Hall's twin, Miller Hall. Upon her own death, in 1939, she donated her entire home, known as the Outlook, to KU for use as the chancellor's residence.

The Outlook is a three-story, twenty-six-room home designed by architect W.J. Mitchell and sports a semicircular porch adorned with Ionic columns and oriel windows along the façade. The second story features a widow's walk providing panoramic views from its location atop Mount Oread. The front elevation faces to the west, toward the university, and is the oldest contributing structure in the University of Kansas East Historic District.

WATSON LIBRARY

1425 Jayhawk Boulevard

When the university opened in 1866, the first library collections were held in Old North College. Located on the north end of Mount Oread, it was the only building on campus, and all faculty offices and classrooms were located here. The literary offerings were modest. Once the university began to expand and built Old Fraser Hall in 1872, the collection expanded as well. In 1894, a donation by William B. Spooner, who happened to be Chancellor Snow's uncle, allowed KU to build Spooner Hall. This new freestanding library offered five times as much space. It was a short-term solution, and when the university's collection expanded, plans were called for to construct a much larger primary library.

Construction began on the Watson Library in the spring of 1923. Named after Carrie Watson, the longest-serving university library at that time, it opened for student use during the fall semester of 1924. Five additions

Before being moved around a variety of campus buildings, the last being Spooner Hall, KU's Watson Library opened in 1924. Its numerous additions have an almost maze-like structure, as it continues to serve as the primary library. *Author's collection.*

were made to Watson between 1938 and 1963, creating an almost maze-like building from the perspective of both students and librarians. As other, more specialized libraries began opening on campus, the state legislature approved a revitalization project in 1978. It continues as the primary library on campus.

STAUFFER-FLINT HALL

1435 Jayhawk Boulevard

Constructed of Oread limestone, this hall was built in 1897–98 through a gift from Kansas City meatpacker and rancher George A. Fowler. Kansas City architects Walter C. Root and George W. Siemens designed the building, setting it apart from its neighbors with a tower at the east end. It was originally designed to serve the university as shops and studios for engineering students. In 1949, a new shop was built to the south of Marvin and Lindley Halls, and this building was remodeled.

In 1952, the School of Journalism and the University Press moved here from the Chemistry and Medical Hall near Watson Library. This department was established in 1909, having been initiated in 1903 by professor and longtime department chair Leon N. Flint, for whom the building was renamed in 1982, along with Oscar Stauffer, the Topeka media mogul and university donor. In 1945, the department was named the William Allen White School of Journalism & Public Information in honor of the KU alumnus and late Emporia publisher and editor. A renovation project in 2019 brought a new plaza, front door and extensive renovations to the first and third floors of the building.

BAILEY HALL

1440 Jayhawk Boulevard

KU's original Chemistry Building was designed for the use of only seventy-five students and, as such, needed a replacement quickly. Constructed in 1900 by former Kansas State Architect John Haskell, this Romanesque building gave the university enough room for the expansion of the department and allowed for the best practical conditions for chemical and pharmaceutical work; KU became one of the first universities to invest in that kind of research, and the program attained national distinction. Among several scientific breakthroughs made in the building, in 1905, KU chemistry professors Hamilton B. Cady and David F. McFarland discovered helium in natural gas.

Known originally as Chemistry Hall, the building took on its new name in 1935, being named officially for KU Professor of Chemistry E.H.S. Bailey, following years of it being informally known as "Bailey's Barn." Despite Bailey's scientific background, he was the one who developed the famous "Rock Chalk, Jayhawk, KU" chant. In 1954, the chemistry department moved to the new Malott Hall while Bailey underwent renovations for the next two years. Following the renovation, the School of Education called Bailey home for another forty-four years. Chemistry has long moved out of Bailey; in its place moved departments in humanities and the social sciences.

WESCOE HALL

1445 Jayhawk Boulevard

With the university facing a quickly expanding student population in 1966, it realized that it was running out of space. The university secured money to construct a new building that would bring together the scattered humanities departments under one roof on the site of the original Haworth Hall and Robinson Gymnasium. Initial plans called for a twenty-five-story skyscraper, with attached five-story wings, all of which would be accompanied with a 150-space parking garage (which would later lead to rumors that Wescoe was a refurbished garage). The cost for the project was too high, and facing the expiration of federal funds, KU had to scale back the project until, ultimately, it became a four-story building. Classes began in April 1973, a year prior to its completion and dedication, which came on April 20, 1974. It was named in honor of Chancellor W. Clarke Wescoe (1960–69) and is the central hub for humanities on campus. The modernist concrete structure remains a center of campus activity, as well as a target for some mockery on campus to this day. However, Wescoe Beach, the ironically named concrete front yard, is constantly in use throughout the year as a popular spot for Greek life and activity recruiting, tabling and campus life.

STRONG HALL

1450 Jayhawk Boulevard

Strong Hall stands as one of the largest and most distinctive historic buildings on campus. Constructed in three phases over a period of a dozen years, from 1911 to 1923, Strong Hall anchors the center of the university, serving as the main administration building for KU. Originally called the "Administrative Building" in 1934, it was named for Frank Strong, who was chancellor from 1902 to 1920 and was known as a proponent for a new administration building as part of the university's first campus master plan. His hope was that it would ease overcrowding at Fraser Hall. Unfortunately, the state legislature did not approve enough funding to complete the building in one fell swoop, and the original design by Kansas City architect George Kessler was drastically scaled back.

The East Wing was completed in 1911, and the West Wing followed in 1918. World War I delayed the project and eventually saw cadets training

Strong Hall, KU's administrative building, is seen here on June 8, 1918, during the construction of its west wing. The building wouldn't be completed until 1923. *Courtesy of the University of Kansas Archives.*

at the West Wing's construction side, utilizing the construction trenches to prepare for the conditions that they might face in Europe. Following the war, construction of the center portion, connecting the two wings, resumed. It was finished in 1923–24, three years following Chancellor Strong's death. University administration personnel moved from Fraser Hall to the new building during the 1923 Christmas break, and construction finally ended less than a month later.

SNOW HALL

1460 Jayhawk Boulevard

Frank Snow was one of the first three faculty members at KU. The renowned scientist and field worker led the acquisition of a vast collection of specimens known as the Snow Entomological Collection, originally held in old Fraser Hall. As the student body grew and the campus looked at expansion, a new building was needed. In 1885, Snow, now chancellor, obtained funds from the state for the construction of a new building to hold the collection and classrooms. Snow Hall was completed in 1886 and was located on the northwest corner of present-day Watson Library. However, after just thirty years, the building suffered from structural issues due to a loose foundation.

Additionally, it was infested with rats and insects and was poorly insulated for either summer or winter. As it was deemed unsafe by Chancellor Strong, the building was closed for use in 1916. Construction on a new Snow Hall began in 1928, and it was dedicated on June 8, 1930, with the old Snow Hall razed in 1934. Additions came in 1950 and 1958, with a significant renovation coming in 1989–90 that saw much of the 1958 addition converted to modern classrooms, offices and additional space for the Snow Entomological Collection, which is now part of the Biodiversity Institute. Today, Snow Hall is home to the departments of math and economics.

BUDIG HALL

1455 Jayhawk Boulevard

KU's basketball program has been a hot commodity for more than a century. As the team grew in popularity during the 1920s, the fan base outgrew their home in Robinson Gymnasium, where the team had played since 1907. As a result, KU constructed Hoch Auditorium, which was designed to serve as a home court, event venue and lecture hall. Completed in 1927 as University Auditorium, it was renamed in 1929 after former Kansas Governor and Board of Regents member Edward W. Hoch. The basketball teams would move out of Hoch and into the new fieldhouse in 1955. For forty years, it hosted the Rock Chalk Revue and was a popular location for student activities. The site has hosted the likes of Steve Martin, John F. Kennedy and Bob Marley.

Concerns about the flammability of Hoch were present ever since construction started, but the state's fire inspector quashed them. Later additions included large wooden roof supports, highly flammable curtains and the use of Celotex (which contained asbestos) as an insulator for enhanced acoustics. To counteract this, the university decided to add lightning rods to the roof. Days before the improvements could begin, lightning struck the building, setting it ablaze on June 15, 1991. All that survived was the front façade. When the university reconstructed the building, located on the former site of Hoch, it became Budig Hall. This was incorporated into the structure, bringing together the old and new to show KU's resilience. It was dedicated on Halloween 1997 and named after Chancellor Gene Budig, the last president of MLB's American League.

MARVIN HALL

1465 Jayhawk Boulevard

Marvin Hall, dedicated on February 25, 1910, is home to the School of Architecture and Design and once housed the School of Engineering until it moved to Learnard Hall in 1963. After engineering left, a 1967 remodel outfitted Marvin Hall for the study of architecture, and it was renamed the School of Architecture and Urban Design in 1968. Renovations came again in the mid-1970s and again in the summer of 2014, when the Marvin Hall Forum was completed. This addition consists of a lecture hall, a common room and a variety of private presentation spaces. The state-of-the-art facility was designed by Studio 804, KU's student architecture group.

Chancellor Frank Strong recognized that KU needed new facilities as it headed into the twentieth century, for class sizes and also for spaces to conduct research. He was refused funds in 1904 but managed to secure them in 1906 for the construction of an engineering building, a mineralogy building (old Haworth Hall), a power plant and other campus projects. Construction began on Marvin Hall in the fall of 1907 and was completed the following year. Because the new power plant was unfinished and could not yet heat the new building, it sat empty for a full year, finally hosting classes in the fall semester of 1909. It was named for Frank O. Marvin, the university's first dean of engineering and the son of James Marvin, the university's third chancellor.

CALIFORNIA-OREGON TRAILS MEMORIAL

1345 West Campus Road

Located on the west side of main campus, near the Chi Omega fountain, there is a large boulder. It denotes the location of the California and Oregon Trails, which run through campus and across Mount Oread. The boulder features a plaque and medallion commemorating the settlers who embarked westward in the nineteenth century. The trail began at various points throughout history, with Independence, Missouri, being the largest and most common starting point. Travelers would trek up the southern slope of Mount Oread, with one branch of the trail passing here. Many settlers would spend the night atop Mount Oread before descending. It passed through this part of campus through the late 1860s, as trail traffic declined due to the Civil War and the construction of the transcontinental railroad. Numerous other trail sites and markers can be found throughout Douglas County.

CHI OMEGA FOUNTAIN

1345 West Campus Road

Located at the western end of Jayhawk Boulevard, the Chi Omega fountain stands as a memorial to the alumni of KU's Lambda Chapter. The project began in October 1952 as part of the sorority chapter's fiftieth anniversary. Half of the cost came from students and alumni, while the rest was paid through KU Endowment's Elizabeth M. Watkins Fund. The limestone fountain was dedicated on April 23, 1955, with three hundred people in attendance. Panels of the fountain feature Greek mythological characters crafted by fine arts student James Bass. Since its construction, the fountain has become a campus landmark due to its location, and it's a popular spot for campus pranks, such as placing dye, soap and even a catfish inside its waters.

POTTER LAKE

Memorial Drive

Construction on Potter Lake began in 1910. For more than a century, Potter Lake has remained a fixture of the university's landscape. Dedicated in 1911 to State Senator and former Board of Regents member Thomas J. Potter, the lake has changed over the years. Sitting on the northern slope of Memorial Drive, it is near the Campanile and Memorial Stadium. The initial purpose behind the lake was to extinguish fires that broke out on campus, and it included a dam, spillways and a bridge. An electric pump and motor system were installed in the lake, with the ability to pump more than one thousand gallons of water per minute. Its pump house, constructed of bricks and limestone, currently sits unused. It covered roughly two acres at the dedication, and at sixteen to eighteen feet in depth, Potter Lake has shrunk significantly over the years.

The lake has featured several activities and props over the years. In 1914, a diving board was erected, briefly; it also briefly was featured as part of a seven-hole campus golf course, since removed. It has served as a classroom for numerous departments, is a popular resting place for students and has housed fish, including one forty-one-inch, twenty-five-

This view of KU, taken in 1913, looks north from campus toward Potter Lake. *Courtesy of the Library of Congress.*

pound flathead catfish that was caught. It has been dredged two times, the first in 1958 due to its polluted nature and again in 2011 to celebrate its centenary anniversary. It has become a receptacle for goal posts from Memorial Stadium as well. After defeating rivals, most recently in 2023 versus Oklahoma, the student body and other fans have pulled the goal post out and hauled it to Potter Lake.

KOREAN WAR MEMORIAL

Memorial Drive

The Korean War Memorial, dedicated in April 2005, was potentially inspired by the old Korean legend viewing cranes as symbols of peace, serenity and nobility. It features four intertwined cranes, each symbolizing the countries involved in the war: South and North Korea, the United States and China. The centerpiece is a six-foot brass crane sculpture by Jon Havener titled *Korean Cranes Rising*; only five legs support the cranes, in that each entity lost a leg through battle, while the fifth represents those KU students who lost their lives in the conflict. Efforts to create the monument date back to the 1990s, but they were spurred by a large donation by KU alum Yong L. Kim Ross in 2003.

The monument incorporates the names of sixty-four members of the KU community who lost their lives, including Jack A. Davenport. During

the dedication ceremony, Chancellor Robert Hemenway told Davenport's story. The KU student saved the lives of his fellow marines by using his body to protect them from a grenade thrown into the foxhole shared by his squad.

MEMORIAL CAMPANILE AND CARILLON

1450 Memorial Drive

The push for a campus carillon tower came from Olin Templin, a KU graduate who had returned in 1890 to establish what are now the departments of philosophy, sociology and psychology. Additionally, he would serve as the executive secretary of the KU Endowment Association. Templin originally wished to construct the carillon tower to honor the pioneers of Lawrence, especially those who suffered during the Civil War. He managed to secure a site and funding for its construction. However, Templin died in 1943, after which the plans began to fade.

With World War II ending, there was a new opportunity to refocus on the tower, resurrected by the KU Memorial Association Committee. Construction on the tower began in 1950 using Kansas limestone. The bells were commissioned from the John Taylor bell foundry in England. On May 27, 1951, the Campanile was dedicated to honor the 277 students who died in the war. The east and west walls of the Memorial Room, located at the base,

A monument to the pioneer settlers of Lawrence was the nascent idea for the Memorial Campanile and Carillon. By the time the project moved forward, World War II had just ended and attention was refocused on the monument. The tower was dedicated in 1951 and is a site of local revery and lore for graduating students. *Author's collection.*

have the names of those 277 Jayhawks. The doors hold reliefs depicting war scenes, inspiration, inscriptions and depictions of other Kansas memories. Inside the Campanile is a carillon, an instrument of fifty-three large bells that resides at the top of the tower. During graduation, students march through the opening of the Campanile on the way to Memorial Stadium for commencement. Legend has it that if a student walks under the Campanile prior to graduation, they will fail to graduate in only four years.

SPENCER ART MUSEUM

1301 Mississippi Street

Sallie Casey Thayer, a Kansas City art collector, donated her collection of more than seven thousand works of art, consisting primarily of art from Asia and Europe, to the University of Kansas in 1917. She made the donation so the university could establish a museum that would encourage the study of fine arts in the Midwest. KU established the University of Kansas Museum of Art in 1928, utilizing Thayer's collection as the basis of the museum, hosting it within Spooner Hall. By the 1960s, under Director Marilyn Stokstad, the museum had quickly outgrown its space.

Another Kansas City collector, Helen Foresman Spencer, made a substantial contribution to fund the construction of a new space in 1978. Designed by architect and KU alum (1926) Robert E. Jenks in the Neoclassical style, it was constructed of Indiana limestone. The museum was renamed in honor of the donor as the Spencer Museum of Art. Only three people have led the museum since that time, the most recent being Saralyn Reece Hardy.

The museum grew by more than nine thousand objects in 2007. The KU Museum of Anthropology collection, which included a wide variety of global cultural materials, many of which were Native American materials, was transferred into its possession. A renovation project followed nearly a decade later in 2016. In addition to transforming the museum space, the project added the Stephen H. Goddard Study Center and the Jack and Lavon Brosseau Center of Learning. The fourth-floor galleries were closed to the public in 2021 for renovation. Today, the museum houses more than forty-eight thousand objects through a variety of media, including American and European art from the ancient to contemporary eras, as well as from a variety of periods of Asian art.

MEMORIAL STADIUM

1101 Mississippi Street

Memorial Stadium, KU's famed football stadium, is one of several war memorials on campus. In the early years, the team played their games on McCook Field, now the site of the David Booth Kansas Memorial

Stadium. In more than 130 years of college football, the Jayhawks played in the 1948 and 2008 Orange Bowl, won the Bluebonnet Bowl in 1961 and saw Ray Evans and Otto Schnellbacher earn the program's first All-American honors. Throughout McCook Field and Memorial Stadium's history, twenty-five players have been inducted into the Kansas Football Ring of Honor, including running back Gale Sayers, quarterback John Hadl and cornerback Aqib Talib. They have appeared in thirteen bowl appearances and have racked up nearly six hundred victories.

The KU Jayhawks played their inaugural season in 1890; captained by Howard Peairs, the team fought through three games that season. Three years later, Ed Harvey became KU's first African American to play football, earning his letters as a member of the team. In fact, he was a multi-sport threat for KU, and opponents found him on the gridiron following stints with the baseball team in 1890 and 1891. The Jayhawks would finish out the nineteenth century with a perfect 10-0 record in 1899, led by College Football Hall of Fame coach Fielding H. Yost. Following a rally against Nebraska, students and faculty were spurred to raise money to build a new concrete stadium. On May 10, 1921, four thousand students showed up on Stadium Day to help demolish old McCook Field.

MURPHY HALL

1530 Naismith Drive

The five-level Murphy Hall was constructed in 1957 and is home to KU's School of Music and School of the Arts. It was named after Franklin Murphy, chancellor from 1952 to 1960, who was a strong advocate for the arts on campus and at state and national levels. Inspired by the performance halls at the new facilities on the campuses of the Universities of Texas and Arkansas, it was constructed after the chancellor promised Thomas Gorton, the new School of Music dean, a new facility. Much of the money spent during construction was spent on the size of the building and on aesthetics rather than acoustics or functionality. This led to several renovations over the years. Today, there are numerous performance spaces housed in Murphy Hall, with the ability to host more than three hundred performances annually. This includes the Crafton-Preyer Theater for plays, musicals, operas and concerts; Swarthout Recital Hall for lectures and solo or small group performances; the Robert F. Baustian Theater, which serves as the university's black-box theater; the William Inge Memorial for lectures, plays and university showcases, named after the well-decorated 1935 theater alum best known for *Picnic* and *Splendor in the Grass*; plus a handful of rehearsal spaces throughout.

KU POWERHOUSE

900 Sunnyside Avenue

The university's powerhouse dates to the early 1880s. During KU's infancy, the campus was powered and heated by steam and coal-burning machinery that was housed in a building right in the middle of campus. The university replaced it with a new boiler house and engine room in 1887, located in a more discreet location. Designed by John G. Haskell and built from Oread limestone quarried on site, the three-story powerhouse featured brick smokestacks and ten decorative arches on its southern façade—six on the first floor and four on the second story.

Significant fires nearly destroyed the building in 1989 and 1990. When the Fowler Shops were constructed, the machine shops were moved there (now Stauffer-Flint Hall), and in 1922, a new powerhouse was constructed on Sunflower Road, placing the old powerhouse into use primarily as storage. In 2002, it was announced that the old structure was going to be modernized, expanded and completely renovated to be the new home for the Hall Center for the Humanities, all while preserving the iconic decorative stone arches. The Hall Center moved from the 1937 Watkins Nursing Home in 2005 and promotes academic research and interdisciplinary communication and collaboration.

ALLEN FIELDHOUSE

1651 Naismith Drive

Allen Fieldhouse is considered one of the most venerated college basketball venues in the country, as well as being one of the most difficult to play in due

Located inside Allen Fieldhouse is the Booth Family Hall of Athletics. Transcending basketball, the hall serves as a history museum of Jayhawk sports. The original banner, made from shower curtains, also read, "Pay Heed, All Who Enter: Beware of the Phog." *Author's collection.*

to a massive home court advantage. It opened on March 1, 1955, and was named for Forrest C. "Phog" Allen, the longtime coach who also played for and was trained by James Naismith, after whom the court is named. After the basketball team formed, the Jayhawks played in several venues, including skating rinks. The university eventually constructed Robinson Gymnasium in 1907 for the team and later Hoch Auditorium, where games were played from 1927 to 1955. Robinson eventually was razed in the late 1960s.

Since its inception, the fieldhouse has been renovated several times and contains the Booth Family Hall of Athletics, a historical exhibition on all Jayhawk sports. Hanging from its rafters high above the court are banners from the NCAA championships in 1922, 1923, 1952, 1988, 2008 and 2022, as well as the women's basketball team's WNIT championship in 2023, along with banners of prominent men and women's basketball players. Above all these banners is one more reading "Pay Heed, All Who Enter: Beware of the Phog." Originally constructed out of dorm room shower curtains before a game in 1988 versus the Duke Blue Devils, this is a more durable version, with the original on display in the Hall of Athletics. Adjacent to the fieldhouse is the DeBruce Center, which contains Naismith's "13 Original Rules of Basket Ball" on display.

CRUTCHFIELD SCHOOLHOUSE

2100 Clinton Parkway

Operating from 1924 to 1959, the Crutchfield School, or Schoolhouse No. 6, is located near the intersection of Clinton Parkway and Iowa Streets, adjacent to some of KU's sports fields. Originally located out in the country, it was soon after located about two miles west of Lawrence's city limits. The first school building here was a simple log school cabin. Later, a larger wood framed building, with two front doors, was completed that seated forty-eight students. This building was demolished in 1924 to provide space for the brick structure seen here today. Crutchfield No. 6 was consolidated with another school in 1959, thus forming the new school of Wakarusa Valley School District No. 98. The building is now a facility of the university.

PIONEER CEMETERY

Constant Avenue and Irving Hill Road

Claimed by homesteader Aaron Perry in 1854, this section of land was settled on the outskirts of town. His family eventually permitted their neighbors to bury their dead within part of their land claim. This led to the creation of a memorial cemetery, originally known as Oread Cemetery. Between 1854 and the 1860s, there was no real system in place for recording the location and the names of those deceased being buried. This was especially true following the deaths of eighteen Union soldiers who died of typhoid in 1862 and the mass killing of civilians by Quantrill's raiders in 1863.

As the city began growing out of Pioneer Cemetery and the university campus started encroaching, many of Quantrill's victims were reburied at Oak Hill Cemetery on the east side of town, although four remain here. While there remain noteworthy figures from the period, the center of the cemetery is marked by an obelisk that honors the martyred antislavery pioneer Thomas Barber. Barber was slain on the eastern outskirts of Lawrence in part due to his stance on the slavery issue. Barber was quickly immortalized by poet John Greenleaf Whittier. Nearby are headstones that honor the eighteen Union soldiers who perished of typhoid fever and serve as a general memorial to the unknown Union soldiers during the Civil War.

Pioneer Cemetery contains the grave and monument to Thomas Barber. The obelisk honors the martyred antislavery settler who was killed outside town. The adjacent slabs contain John Greenleaf Whittier's poem "The Burial of Barber." *Author's collection.*

Eventually, Oread Cemetery fell into disuse, and the city took it over, renaming it in 1928 as Pioneer Cemetery. Repairs and maintenance were spotty over the next forty years. However, that changed in May 1968. Elmer V. McCollum, a KU alum who discovered vitamins A and D and had grown up near the cemetery, requested his ashes be placed in the cemetery. Since that time, the cemetery has become a part of the university campus, restored and maintained by the Historic Mount Oread Fund through KU endowment. McCollum brought new attention to the cemetery. Since his ashes were spread, more than 450 faculty and staff members have been interred at the cemetery, including chancellors, professors and administrators.

THE ROBERT J. DOLE INSTITUTE OF POLITICS

2350 Petefish Drive

More commonly referred to simply as the Dole Institute, the Robert J. Dole Institute of Politics is officially nonpartisan. It pays homage to longtime Kansas Senator Bob Dole (1969–96) and member of the House of Representatives (1961–69). In 1996, he was defeated by Bill Clinton during

The Dole Institute is located on KU's western edge, just past the Lied Center. Officially nonpartisan in focus, it pays homage to the long-serving Kansas Senator Bob Dole. An alum of the university, Dole donated his Congressional papers to the school, and the institute, created to promote civic participation, was born. *Author's collection.*

his Republican bid for the presidency. Dole was notable for crossing party lines to compromise to get the best outcome for his constituents.

Plans for developing the institute began in 1996. Following his loss in the election, Dole was asked by KU Chancellor Robert Hemenway to donate his Congressional papers to the school, as Dole was an alum. He agreed, and thus was born the impetus for the institute, which was created to foster the idea of a political career as one of service and goodwill and to promote civic participation.

MAX KADE ANNEX

1120 West 11th Street

The stone Max Kade Annex is the oldest structure on campus, dating back to 1862. The abolitionist Senator James Lane was the structure's first owner. Lane owned this property and built this stone stable at the highest point on his land. Following James Lane's suicide, the property passed through multiple generations of owners. In 1927, the property was purchased by Mervin Sudler from the School of Medicine. He built a limestone house

Today, it serves as the Max Kade Annex, but this structure dates back to 1862, when James Lane was its first owner. Lane owned the property and constructed this stone stable at the highest point he could find on his land. *Author's collection.*

forty yards from the stable and used it as a garage. When he died in 1956, he bequeathed the house and garage to the university.

In 1975, a group of KU students decided to start a new student-run radio station, KJHK (90.7 FM), and moved into the Annex, giving it the name "The Shack." Unfortunately, The Shack couldn't keep up with ADA standards or code, and the cost to achieve this was out of the question. In 2012, the Max Kade Center moved into the Sudler House, took advantage of the empty annex and renamed it the Max Kade Annex. They were able to undertake the renovations but, in the process, painted over The Shack's iconic garage door art and graffiti. It is now a home for history at KU, holding archival materials of the American Turners New York, a German American society. Dr. Frank Baron, former director of the Max Kade Center for German American Studies, began a historic tracing of the building, leading to James Lane. A plaque was completed in 2016, but it sits at the Watkins Museum of History.

OFF CAMPUS

As campus grew, and continues to grow, housing located near campus became paramount for those working at, and attending, the University of Kansas. Much like the historic neighborhoods of Oread, Old West Lawrence and Babcock Place, abutting campus, those areas to the west and north of campus contain vibrant neighborhoods as well. While maybe not quite as old and historic overall as some of the other areas listed in this book, several historic homes and structures abound nearby in neighborhoods like Schwegler, Centennial, West Hills, the historic Breezedale neighborhood and beyond. Breezedale, marked by a pair of stone and concrete pillars and adjacent to Haskell Indian Nations University, was the city's first attempt to create a suburban neighborhood in 1909–10. Out just a bit farther, beyond the KU campus and Haskell, on the far northern portions of Lawrence, Kansas, much of the land stands as open fields, farmland, wetlands and more rural stretches of neighborhoods.

DAVIS CEMETERY

3526 West 6th Street

Located west of downtown along 6th Street was the farmstead of George Burt and later Henry T. Davis. In the 1850s and 1860s, this location was

Top: The Breezedale entry is just as historic as the homes within this first suburban Lawrence subdivision. When it was developed, the city's streetcar system traveled along Mass Street from downtown to the neighborhood. *Author's collection.*

Bottom: Nestled in the back of a parking lot, next to a neighborhood off of 6th Street, is the farm cemetery of George Burt. Establishing the farmstead in the 1850s along the California Trail, Burt was a victim of the 1863 raid. His relative Henry T. Davis bought the farm and buried his family here. *Author's collection.*

well outside the city limits of Lawrence. The farm cemetery is located on what was once part of the California Trail. These types of cemeteries were common in east Kansas during the settlement period. George Burt was a victim of Quantrill's Raid and was buried here on his family's farm in 1863. A relative of his, Henry T. Davis, then bought out the farm and buried his family here. Today, it sits in between a commercial parking lot and a residential street.

CHEWNING HOUSE

1510 Stratford Road

Located in the West Hills neighborhood, west of campus, this home was built for Helen and Bert Chewning, the superintendent of the university post office. Designed by the chair of the KU architecture program, George M. Beal, it was one of a thousand "New American Home" properties erected during the Great Depression by the FHA and General Electric. At the time of its construction, an all-electric home was still an innovation, and it stood as one of the first modern homes built in town, starting a new Lawrence rejuvenation, last seen after the Civil War.

GE and the FHA began working together on a design contest that would get turned into an actual house. The winners were incorporated into the program's first "New American Home." The project drew in visitors when it traveled on display and gained notoriety for homes with all-electric features to provide comfort and convenience. During the second year of the program, the Chewnings' house came to prominence. It was Lawrence's only home in the program, and in the first two days open as a model, more than 1,300 people visited. The home included such innovations as scientific lighting, GE appliances (e.g., dishwashers, garbage disposals, radios and more) and electric heating and cooling. Planners intended to utilize it as a more modern approach to community planning. A resulting boom in construction was expected, but World War II put a pause on that, especially in the field of all-electric homes. This home became the precursor to Lawrence's era of modern architecture from 1945 to 1970.

FERDINAND-STRONG HOUSE

1515 University Drive

Likely the most famous person to have lived in this house was neither a Ferdinand nor a Strong—James Naismith, inventor of the game of basketball, owned the house in his later years, dying here in 1939. However, it was KU Chancellor Frank Strong who gave the home part of its name, as he lived here prior to Naismith, from 1919 to 1934. The main portion of the wood-frame Italianate home—replete with a stone-lined cellar, an imposing tower and slender windows—was constructed around 1872 for J.J. and Cyrena Fernand along Mount Oread's ridge. The home changed hands nearly a dozen times until just after the turn of the century. A large addition was added in 1905. In May 1908, the home was rented by the university from Castle Spencer and used as the first student hospital for KU, before it moved on-campus later in the year.

Inventor of basketball Dr. James Naismith, seen here in the 1930s holding a peach basket and basketball, lived in Lawrence, dying at home in 1939. *Courtesy of the Library of Congress.*

When Dr. Strong retired, he moved from his campus home to this one. Strong and his wife, Mary, lived here until his death in 1934. Mary sold the house to Coach Naismith in March 1939, remaining there until his death in November that year. His widow rented the home to students during World War II and sold the property in 1947; the city annexed it later that year. The new owners were professors of fine art and music, Raymond and Alberta Stuhl. They provided music lessons from their home for five decades, owning the home until their deaths in 1994 and 2000, respectively. While none of the original outbuildings remains, a garage was added in 2003.

BEAL-CHARLTON HOUSE

1624 Indiana Street

Topeka native George Malcolm Beal designed and lived in this home during his tenure in the architecture program at KU. His influence would shape the transition of the program from classical to modern styles. Beal taught nonclassical architectural courses in 1928, the first to do so academically nationwide before joining Frank Lloyd Wright in 1934 as an honorary Taliesin Fellow. It led to a lifelong friendship between the two. Beal, as a practicing architect and full-time professor, became an innovator in solar energy being used in residential architecture. Later, he would chair the architecture department and later act as its director.

He designed this home during this time in 1950. Utilizing and expanding on Wright's Usonian design principles, he engineered the home to take full advantage of solar gain. It was so successful that he claimed he could leave the boiler off on winter days because the windows and the shed roof allowed the sun to effectively heat the home. Betty Jo Charlton, KU's first female engineering student and the city's first woman legislator, purchased the home, living there from 1971 to 2014. She had drafted for Boeing in Wichita during World War II, received degrees in engineering and political science at KU and was appointed to fill a vacant seat in the Kansas House. She went on to serve seven more terms before retiring. Betty died in the home, as she wished, at the age of ninety-one.

CORDLEY ELEMENTARY SCHOOL

1837 Vermont Street

Cordley Elementary School is the oldest elementary school still in operation in Lawrence. Established in 1915, the school opened its doors in 1916. Standing at two stories in height and facing 19th Street, it sits on just shy of 3.5 acres. The school is named for Reverend Richard Cordley, an abolitionist minister and survivor of the 1863 raid. Cordley helped rebuild the town and served on the city's board of education for seven years, serving as its president for six years.

The school has undergone a series of changes over the years. In 1928, an additional floor was added to the top of the original structure. In 1950, the main entrance was pivoted away from 19th Street to face Vermont Street. That year, classrooms and a combination gymnasium and lunchroom were added to the east and north of the original building. Four additional classrooms were added five years later. The old gym was converted into a media center in 1996, with a new gymnasium and kitchen added as well. Most recently, in 2014, the school shut down, moving its students to East Heights in order to accommodate an extensive restoration project. The main entrance was returned to the original south entrance, the original wood floors in the office received a re-staining and polishing and new cafeterias, learning pockets, elevator and a new kitchen-cafeteria were added.

LAWRENCE HIGH SCHOOL

1901 Louisiana Street

For more than 160 years, Lawrence High School has had just as strong a history in sports in Lawrence as have the Jayhawks. The Chesty Lions have won more than one hundred sports championships and sport an illustrious list of alumni. Lawrence High School was the city's first and largest high school. This high school stood as the only one until 1997, when Free State High School opened on the west side of town. They would move into the new Liberty Memorial High School following World War I, with the building serving as a monument to students lost during the war. In 1949, a drive to build a more modern building was initiated. The high school was moved from Liberty Memorial High School at 14th and Massachusetts to this location on March 26, 1954; the old building was converted into a middle school. Expanded facilities and improvements came in 1973, 1989, 1995, 2005 and through the 2007–08 and 2008–09 school years. On-site sports facilities were added during the last phase and included a football stadium, a new track, a soccer field, baseball and softball fields and tennis courts.

Notable alumni featured in the schools Hall of Honor include pro football player John Hadl, basketball great Danny Manning, All-American Paul Endacott, author Sara Paretsky, baseball player and manager Ralph Houk, broadcaster Hank Booth, former Kansas Governor Robert Docking, author and illustrator Stephen Johnson, sculptor Elden Tefft, advocate Erin Pattee Brockovich-Ellis, singer-songwriter and founder of the band BR549 Chuck Mead, cartoonist Paul Coker (who created the school's Chesty Lion mascot illustration) and founding member of the band Kansas Robert "Robby" Steinhardt.

DOUBLE HYPERBOLIC PARABOLOID HOUSE

934 West 21st Street

Located south of KU, this home was designed by Donald Dean, professor of civil engineering at the university from 1955 to 1960, along with the help of his students. This home is the first mid-century residence to be listed in the National Register of Historic Places and the Kansas Historic Register, having been listed successfully in 2006 by its owners. Dean was looking to construct an inexpensive home that could be constructed during the 1950s housing boom and was relatively affordable.

The double hyperbolic paraboloid house was designed by civil engineer professor Donald Dean with the help of his students. The home was controversial when constructed and has received much attention over the years. *Author's collection.*

Dean looked at Spanish architect Felix Candela's work. Candela had constructed several homes in Mexico that featured a reinforced concrete paraboloid roof. Dean figured that this sort of roof for mass production would be cost-prohibitive. However, as an alternative, he experimented with wood lattice instead as the basic material; then he found a way to construct it quickly and inexpensively with plywood sheets.

At the time of its construction, the home was controversial. Many found it too radical, although others admired the lines and slopes of the roof as being a graceful addition. Regardless, it became a unique addition to the neighborhood. Inside, a squat twenty-three-foot-wide brick fireplace serves as the living room's focal point, strafed by a plunging ceiling. The home is also filled with light on the north and east sides of the homes with its floor-to-ceiling glass windows. On the west side of the home, however, no walls even meet the ceiling.

GEORGE W. GOSS HOUSE

1101 21st Street

George W. Goss was among the first party of settlers to arrive in Lawrence, under the aegis of the New England Emigrant Aid Society, in 1854. As such, Goss and his property operated as safe spots along the Underground Railroad. This brick Federal-style home was constructed by Goss in 1870–71, well after the end of the Civil War. It is a part of the Owens Lane Addition, the first custom mid-century subdivision in Lawrence. Being located on the outskirts of town offered additional protection, as bounty hunters still traveled into Kansas to capture slaves as well as round up additional free Blacks to sell as slaves.

DINE-O-MITE INN

23rd and Louisiana Streets

Prior to the 1950s, Lawrence was, like almost all other American towns, segregated. Most white people in Lawrence, including famed basketball coach Phog Allen, accepted racial segregation. However, his mind changed when he started recruiting Wilt Chamberlain to the Jayhawks, and he began urging local businesses to end the practice. Chamberlain arrived in Lawrence right in the midst of the Montgomery Bus Boycott. Known throughout the country for his basketball prowess, Chamberlain was aware of his celebrity status and decided to use it to push for integration.

Wilt would frequently go to the leading restaurants in Lawrence near campus, all practicing racial segregation. The owners refused to serve African Americans, but Wilt was a celebrity and everyone in town knew that the team depended on him. The restaurant owners figured that they could not anger Chamberlain, as he might leave, and the other players and fans would follow. If Wilt were there, well, others would want to be there as well, and that included Dine-O-Mite. Wilt managed to befriend the owners, and they eventually softened their stance on race. While Wilt refused to participate in sit-ins, most athletes at the time tried to avoid controversy altogether. His actions showed that it was possible for white and Black people to dine together in Lawrence.

Wilt Chamberlain is seen here flipping through records during his thirty-minute weekly show *Flip'er with Dipper* inside the KUOK radio station sometime during 1955–58, while he was a student at KU. *Courtesy of the University of Kansas, University Archives.*

SAVAGE HOME

1734 Kent Terrace

This home was built in 1855 by one of Lawrence's earliest settlers, and early city band member, Joseph Savage. It is believed to be the oldest home still standing in town. A farmer, Joseph was also a staunch abolitionist, as were many of the early settlers in town. During the family's first two years in town, Joseph's wife and four of his five children perished. When Quantrill's raiders swept through town in 1863, Joseph was there. He managed to survive, later finding his cornet damaged in the debris from the raid. He would have it repaired and go on to perform with the city band for years.

Savage, an avid amateur scientist, allowed his home to become a gathering place for the new university leaders. Despite not receiving a college education himself, he was granted membership in the university's Science Club and would frequently host events at his home for the club, which has been credited with the famous "Rock Chalk, Jayhawk" chant that is pervasive to this day.

The home was supposedly the first wood-frame home built in Douglas County. The small room on the back side of the house once served as a living room and still includes the original cracked brick chimney. Even the newer portion of the home is considered historic, as it was built sometime following the Civil War but prior to the end of the 1870s. Located off one of Lawrence's most trafficked intersections, it can be found nestled behind a retail strip center off 23rd and Iowa Streets.

GROVER BARN

2819 Stone Barn Terrace

Joel Grover arrived in Lawrence in 1854 with the New England Emigrant Aid Company's second party. On the northwestern outskirts of town, Joel and his wife, Emily, both staunch abolitionists, purchased land and established a farm, building this stone barn on the property. In addition to serving their farm, this stone barn, which still features the original stone walls and wooden beams despite modifications made over the years, served as a shelter for freedom seekers along the Underground Railroad. This

Joel Grover arrived with the second company of Lawrence settlers. The abolitionist purchased this land and built this stone barn on his farm. It served as a stop on the Underground Railroad, one of several such sites in Lawrence. *Author's collection.*

includes Jim Daniels; his wife, Narcissus; their children; and others. John Brown and his men liberated them from slavery in December from farms in Vernon and Bates Counties, Missouri, in January 1859. During their trek north, Narcissus went into labor and gave birth, naming their son Captain John Brown Daniels. After a short stay to allow Narcissus and the baby time to recover, Brown led the caravan from the barn and headed to Topeka. They headed north along the Lane Trail, encountering opposition during the very brief Battle of the Spurs before moving on to Detroit, from which they passed into Canada in March.

The land was farmed by the Grover family until the 1950s. Following that, a local artist used the barn as a studio; then it served as the city's Fire Station No. 4. The Guardians of Grover Barn has preserved the structure and added three informational kiosk panes that tell the Underground Railroad history of the site, the Grover family and the history of the barn after the Grovers. The Grover Barn is also a designated site on the National Park Service's Underground Railroad Network to Freedom.

BAKER UNIVERSITY WETLANDS AND DISCOVER CENTER

1365 North 1250 Road

Developed by the Wakarusa River's meandering, flooding and sediment deposit, these wetlands have long been a feature of the region that now houses the city of Lawrence. Archaeological digs and studies show that during the pre-Haskell era, this area was used by the Kanza tribe and later tribes that were relocated by the government to this area. Development encroached as settlers moved in as early as 1854. An early map shows a bridge located less than a quarter mile east of the current bridge along Louisiana Street, and travel cuts into the banks can be found in several places. The future of the land—used by Haskell University, local farmers and then the City of Lawrence—was eventually up for development. Instead, the federal government transferred the land to Baker University in 1967, which planned to restore and preserve the area as an educational wetland.

Dr. Ivan Boyd, who oversaw the site, began the wetlands restoration in 1991. Several enhancements were made over the next twenty years, including an information kiosk, an observation blind, educational panels and a map. In September 2008, Baker University started the conversion of 140 acres of cropland and the old Haskell Farm back into wetlands. An additional 310 acres of floodplain crop fields were restored to protect the wetlands, along with the restoration of other land to prairie and native riparian forest. Today, the site is open for exploration, with a discovery center that is open during the week with limited hours (call first if you plan to visit). The Baker Wetlands includes more than eleven miles of trails, open from dawn to dusk.

BLANTON'S TOLL BRIDGE SITE

CR 1400 at the Wakarusa River Bridge

The site of Napoleon Blanton's toll bridge is located near Douglas County Road 1400, spanning the Wakarusa River. Constructed in 1854, it proved to be very popular and profitable, as numerous settlers and travelers passed this way. Numerous notable events occurred here, including a series of events known as the Wakarusa War. This began when proslavery man Frank Coleman shot and killed his abolitionist neighbor Charles Dow over a land dispute. In response, area abolitionists set fire to a number of proslavery cabins. Sheriff Samuel Jones arrived from Westport, Missouri, in response. After he arrived, instead of arresting Coleman, he took abolitionist leader Jacob Branson to Westport. Along the way, an abolitionist posse overtook the sheriff at Blanton's Bridge, freeing Branson. Jones returned to Westport and amassed a force of nearly two thousand Missourians to quell the "insurrection," while abolitionists gathered in Lawrence. John Brown, along with some of his sons, set out as well. When they arrived at Blanton's Bridge, they found a well-armed group of border ruffians who, upon seeing that the Browns were heavily armed, let them pass. Eventually, Territorial Governor Wilson Shannon's intervention and a major ice storm resulted in a truce, bringing the Wakarusa War to an end.

Following the destruction of Lawrence, Quantrill's raiders made their escape, having witnessed from atop Mount Oread the federal soldiers beginning their pursuit. Following Louisiana Street out of Lawrence, they crossed the Wakarusa River at Blanton's Bridge, burning it to evade

Free State supporters, known as Jayhawkers, are seen here standing in front of what is thought to be an abolitionist cabin in the 1850s. *Courtesy of the Library of Congress.*

capture. Blanton and his family hid farther down the river to escape detection from the raiders. Archaeological investigations have taken place at the site, which also includes the ruins of Blanton's stone house. Travelers along the road can see the ruins of Blanton's home near the river.

DOUGLAS COUNTY POOR FARM

East of East 1500 Road and North of North 1175 Road

Poor houses and poor farms were a social institution dating back to 1697. Residents ranged from the sick to vagrants, the blind, the able-bodied poor, unmarried mothers and children. In America's Midwestern states, these homes were run with male residents tending to animals, crops and routine maintenance, while women took care of the house and household chores. The first poor farms in Kansas opened in Leavenworth and Douglas Counties in 1866, and by 1899, 80 of the 105 Kansas counties had one.

Douglas County's poor farm was organized in 1866, following the purchase of a 160-acre farm from George Stearns. The farm was located a little more than a mile south of 31st Street and Haskell Avenue, south of the Wakarusa River. Plans were made for a farmhouse standing two stories high. In 1870, the farm had twelve residents ranging in age from two to eighty years old. The farm's population expanded over the years, and in 1911, new plans called for the construction of a two-story brick structure to replace the old frame house. A fire struck in April 1944, destroying the building and killing eight of the twenty-six residents. A small farmhouse was built in its stead southwest of the poor farm ruins using whatever materials they could salvage. The county sold the livestock and equipment and finally sold the land in 1946. World War II basically ended talks of rebuilding the poor farm completely, but Douglas County still wanted and needed to care for the elderly and bought a house at 1004 West 4th Street to be used as a convalescent hospital. Nothing remains of the Douglas County Poor Farm today except the replacement brick building constructed after the disastrous fire.

OUTSIDE OF TOWN

Founded in August 1855, Douglas County was one of the first counties organized in Kansas. Named after Stephen A. Douglas, the U.S. senator from Illinois who introduced the Kansas-Nebraska Act, the county became a center of turmoil during the Bleeding Kansas period. With antislavery leaders in Lawrence facing the proslavery leaders in Lecompton, the entire country was thrust into the spotlight. Communities abound throughout the county and include cities such as Baldwin City, Eudora, Lecompton and the country seat of Lawrence. Many more unincorporated communities dot the landscape, and there are a handful of ghost towns as well, some of which lie underneath the waters of Clinton Lake.

TOWN OF FRANKLIN

East Hills Drive

Two long neglected and nearly forgotten cemeteries sit in the prairie land just north of Kansas Highway 10. Located four miles southeast of Lawrence, one fenced-in cemetery sits on the east side, serving the non-Catholic population for the town of Franklin, and the other, a Catholic cemetery, is a short distance to the west, across the street. The last known burial occurred in this cemetery in 1914, bringing the total to just over twenty known burials. There are a few other grave markers inside the fenced enclosure, located

Above: Clinton Lake, seen here from the dam above its spillway, was created in 1972. The project destroyed a number of historic territorial settlements, covering them with water. Not much of many of the old communities remain, as they were either demolished, abandoned or flooded. *Author's collection.*

Left: Not much is left of the proslavery town of Franklin. A handful of graves from two cemeteries straddle East Hills Drive on the far east part of town, just north of K-10. *Author's collection.*

on the east side of East Hills Drive, just north of K-10, but it has been abandoned and unmaintained. Across East Hills Drive and a short walk away is the Franklin Catholic Cemetery. It has been restored following years of neglect. The oldest tombstone here is from 1869, and the graveyard contains fifty-two known burials and seventeen stones.

Franklin was founded in October 1853 and quickly became a proslavery stronghold and trading post along the stagecoach route from Westport, Missouri. With Lawrence the unofficial capital of the antislavery movement, the settlers in the two towns were constantly at each other's throats. The Battle of Franklin, in June 1856, featured John Brown leading Free State forces to the settlement in response to the May 21, 1856 sack of Lawrence and the Battle of Fort Saunders that August 12. Additional smaller skirmishes in the years leading up to the war saw the influence of the proslavery town dwindle. Following the Civil War, Franklin quickly declined. Fort Franklin, which housed the Mexican-American War cannon "Old Sacramento," remained for several years as one of the defining and final features of the old settlement.

THE OUTHOUSE

1837 North 1500 Road

The Outhouse, now a strip joint, was a venerated music venue serving the area from 1985 to 1998. Located about four miles east of the city, the Outhouse mainly hosted punk bands like Green Day, Nirvana, Black Flag, Iggy Pop and more. Owner Donny Mellenbruch had been leasing the property for parties but had hosted very few shows. Local band the Micronotz built a stage and cleaned up the concrete building in 1984–85, and Mellenbruch began consistently hosting shows in 1985.

The venue was sparse with only its cinder block walls, stage and concrete floor. It was hot in the summer and cold in the winter and the toilets rarely worked, causing many attendees to head to the surrounding corn fields. Additionally, the shows ended late and noise was common, as was unruly behavior. Shows became less frequent in the 1990s, especially with more venues opening (with working HVAC and plumbing) in town. Following the flood of 1993, things never really returned to normal at the Outhouse. Mellenbruch lost his lease in 1998, closing the Outhouse as a music venue.

Now a strip joint, the Outhouse was a punk rock haven on the east outskirts of town. Artists like Green Day, Nirvana and Iggy Pop have all played at the cinder block and concrete venue. *Author's collection.*

BLUE MOUND

E 1700 Road—Private Property

Trail sites abound in Douglas County near Lawrence. Many trails that originated in the Kansas City area primarily followed the same path until they reached Gardner, Kansas, in southern Johnson County. From here, the Santa Fe Trail headed southwest, while the Oregon and California Trails moved to the east-northeast. By the time travelers reached present-day Douglas County, the Oregon Trail had diverged several miles north of the Santa Fe Trail. One of the earliest major landmarks along the Oregon and California Trails was Blue Mound, located southeast of Lawrence. Despite growth in the area, it is still a visible landmark for quite a distance, but at that time, the land was still open, prairie with trees relegated to the Wakarusa River, making it visible for miles away.

Today, roads surround Blue Mound, allowing people to get near the historic site. The peak rises about 230 feet above the plains surrounding it, and the trail roughly follows the hill's south side timber line. Also known as Mont Bleu, this site was used to receive lantern signals from Signal Oak near Baldwin City, warning of oncoming invaders, and was a relay point to Lawrence's Mount Oread. Unfortunately, it was not being used on August 21, 1863. Following Quantrill's Raid, Union Major Preston B. Plumb arrived at Blue Mound with more than one hundred soldiers but was unsuccessful in encountering and stopping the guerrillas. The raiders headed south past the mound and then scattered in escape. In the 1970s, developers crafted a ski slope and T-bar for winter activities.

BROOKLYN TOWNSITE

Near North 550 and East 1400 Roads

Lawrence was not the only town that got destroyed by William Quantrill on August 21, 1863. Located just fifteen miles southeast of Lawrence, the town of Brooklyn wasn't much to look at; it featured an inn, a saloon and a general store, a stable and a handful of homes. Incorporated in 1858, it served as a trading post along the Santa Fe Trail. Following Quantrill's attack on Lawrence, one of the raider's spotters saw federal troops approaching. The guerrillas hightailed it out of town, heading south on the Fort Scott Road, which intersects with the Santa Fe Trail at Brooklyn.

The settlers had been warned about the approaching raiders and hid as many belongings as possible and fled to the corn fields to hide. Likely running on adrenaline and liquor by this point, and possibly to distract their pursuers, the raiders torched the settlement, except the town saloon, before riding on. There is also a theory that Brooklyn was targeted, and the raiders happened to run past by chance; Brethren leaders Abraham Rothrock and Jacob Ulrich, potentially members of the Underground Railroad, lived here. Rothrock was shot and injured in the melee. Brooklyn stood for only eight years before being destroyed. All that's left are the remains of a few foundations and a historic marker.

WELLS OVERLOOK

1373 North 1000 Road

Numerous places abound to get good views of Lawrence and its surrounding terrain. One of the best, however, is Wells Overlook Park, located roughly

Wells Overlook, which includes a multi-story observation tower, gives a good view of the surrounding countryside, including Lawrence. In recent years, an ADA platform has been added, making the site accessible to all. *Author's collection.*

three miles south of Lawrence. The site includes a pavilion and a multi-story overlook tower. At its highest vantage point, you get great views in three directions, while the pavilion sports interpretive displays that identify various spots along the horizon, including Lawrence and Blue Mound. The park was donated in 1971 to Douglas County by William Wells.

HICKORY POINT

South Side of N600 Road

Prior to being opened to settlement, the area that is now Kansas contained outposts, including one spot on the Santa Fe Trail called Hickory Point. Located about two days' travel from Westport by wagon, by 1854, Hickory Point sported two blacksmith shops, a harness shop, a hotel, a supply store and several homes. It soon became prime settlement land when the territory officially opened.

In November 1855, Charles Dow was shot and killed at Hickory Point. Jacob Branson, Dow's friend and roommate, was erroneously arrested by Sheriff Samuel Jones for murder, leading to the Wakarusa War. Sometime around 1856, the area changed its name to Stony Point, as there was another Hickory Point located about twenty-five miles to the north.

Eventually, when the trails quit being used because of the opening of the transcontinental railroad, Stony Point eventually ceased to exist as a town, but the community remained. Around 1868, they built a rock school roughly a mile east of the townsite, from the Stony Point Farm, which was deeded in August 1860. It would become the focal point of the community, with a cemetery later added to the site. The wood Stony Point Evangelical Lutheran Church was built in 1883 by Henry Obadiah and used until 1900, and no other services, save a few funerals or annual picnic, have been conducted here since.

WAKARUSA RIVER VALLEY HERITAGE MUSEUM

716 North 1190 Road

When the U.S. Army Corps of Engineers announced plans to dam the Wakarusa River west of Lawrence to build Clinton Lake in 1972, residents feared that the history of the area would be washed away by the flooding of the valley, a common occurrence in these projects. As a result of this fear, in 1983 the Wakarusa River Valley Heritage Museum was established. Martha Parker, a lifetime resident of Clinton, assumed a leadership role in the preservation of the history of the region, including the communities of Kanwaka, Stull, New Belvoir, Old Belvoir, Clinton, Bloomington, Sigel, Twin Mount, Richland and Lone Star. Many of these communities were either demolished, abandoned or flooded.

The historical society planned to establish the Clinton Lake Museum in former Bloomington resident Colonel James C. Steele's home, constructed in 1865 by brick made from clay from the Wakarusa River. Unable to be restored, the home was dismantled and fragments preserved for later incorporation into a reconstructed cowshed to be used as the museum. Included in the exhibits are the original windows of the home, S-shaped brick anchors and some of the original red bricks. The exhibits tell the story of the valley, which was involved heavily in the events of Bleeding Kansas and the Civil War. It was a battleground area between the proslavery and Free State factions and housed several stops on the Underground Railroad, including the homes of Ezekial Colman in Kanwaka, Henry Hiatt in Twin Mount and Joseph Gardner in Lone Star.

JOHN KELLY STONE BUILDING

777 North 1750 Road

It is believed that the John Kelley building was constructed in 1874. Outbuildings and wagon ruts from travelers on the California and Oregon Trails are found near the historic farmstead. One can still see the old stone building, remnants of an old windmill and a pump that travelers on the trail would use to obtain water. While John Kelley was the first homeowner, the Willis A. Colman family lived there the longest, residing here from 1902 to 1994.

When Congress passed a bill in 1855 awarding land to former soldiers and officers, it included land in the Great Plains region. In 1960, a deed for a 160-acre farm was given to Mehitable H. Sanders, widow of U.S. Navy officer Samuel Sanders, a veteran of the War of 1812. She would pass the farm on to John Kelly, who began living on the property in 1860. He did not build the home until after the war was over and after Lawrence was in its rebuilding boom, as a date of 1874 is inscribed on the limestone, likely denoting its construction date. Initially, the stone building served as Kelley's home, but the construction of a wooden house allowed him to convert the three-story limestone structure into a chicken coop, blacksmith shop and smokehouse.

Willis Colman, purportedly the first white male born in the county in 1855, purchased the farm in 1902. His kids would maintain the farm following his 1934 death, with his son Willis Ray Colman taking over full ownership in 1940, living in a seven-room house on the property. It was one of three homes to burn on the farm. Following, the property would change hands but stayed in the Colman family until they sold it to the Price family in 1994. A 2013 reconstruction project saved the single-story limestone building, with expert masons dismantling and rebuilding it stone by stone.

LANE UNIVERSITY

319 Elmore Street—Lecompton

Founded in 1865 by Reverend Solomon Weaver and named for its largest donor, Senator James Lane, this university began construction in 1882. The university started in the city's Rowena Hotel but relocated when the state donated thirteen acres that included the foundation of what had been intended to be the Kansas territorial capitol building. The capitol had been completed to the bottom of the first-floor windows when the U.S. House of Representatives defeated the Lecompton Constitution by only eight votes, keeping Kansas from entering the Union as a slave state with Lecompton as its capital. When it became clear that Lecompton would not become the Kansas capital, work ceased on construction. At that time, the foundation for three wings had been laid, the center section had been completed up to the first-floor windows and all the materials to complete it, including four pillars, were lying on the ground. In 1856, the foundation was used as a fortress to stop James Lane from destroying the town and rescue Charles Robinson from jail, who had been tried for treason. In response, they marched south, meeting Colonel Henry Shombre and Captain Samuel Walker at the Battle of Fort Titus at Coon Creek.

Throughout most of its history, the Church of the United Brethren in Christ owned and managed the school building. Two notable students were Ida Stover and David Eisenhower, the parents of former President Dwight D. Eisenhower, who met and married in the university chapel, which has been preserved, in 1885. In 1902, Lane University united with Campbell University to form Campbell College, which closed in 1933. It serves as the city's history museum.

CONSTITUTIONAL HALL

319 Elmore Street—Lecompton

Designed in the Greek Revival style, Constitution Hall was built by Douglas County Sheriff (and proslavery proponent) Samuel Jones in 1856–57. The building was designed to house a U.S. Land Office on the first floor and the District Courthouse on the second floor. It would become one of the busiest locations in the Kansas Territory, as thousands of new territorial settlers arrived to file claims here.

As the territory pushed to become the nation's new state, the Lecompton Constitutional Convention met here to draft the statehood constitution. The events were covered heavily by newspapers across the country, and the seats were filled with reporters.

However, the Lecompton Constitution protected slavery, and there was fear that if the new constitution could not satisfy both sides of the debate, the country would be led into war. Their draft of the constitution ultimately failed, and Kansas was admitted as a Free State in 1861; the country would head to war shortly thereafter regardless. Since the territorial days, Constitution Hall has also served as a dry goods store, undertaker's office, lodge, hotel and dormitory. It has been preserved as a Kansas State Historic Site and is open to the public.

SHERIFF SAMUEL J. JONES MARKER

Elmore Street—Lecompton

Entrepreneur Samuel J. Jones had moved west with his family from Virginia to Westport, Missouri, in 1854. The Kansas Territory had just opened, and Jones, who supported the proslavery cause, got involved in the politics of the time, becoming appointed postmaster of Westport. During the spring of 1855, Jones took a group of proslavery men to Bloomington in Douglas County, Kansas, and destroyed the ballot box during the election cycle. The proslavery government, then led by acting governor and fellow Virginian Daniel Woodson, appointed him as first sheriff of the county on August 27, 1855. In his attempts to enforce the laws of the Kansas legislature, he met resistance, leading to vast outbreaks of violence. He would go on to construct Constitution Hall in 1856, which is now a National Historic Landmark and became the location for Kansas's path to statehood as a Free State.

Jones's time as sheriff wasn't extensive; he ceded his position on January 7, 1857, instead of creating a more lenient approach suggested by Territorial Governor John W. Geary. Jones moved his family to New Mexico, where he purchased a ranch, living there until his 1883 death. His tombstone was transported in 2013 to Lecompton, where it now lies near Constitution Hall.

DEMOCRATIC HEADQUARTERS

East Second Street—Lecompton

Constructed in the 1850s by Italian stonemason Mark Migliario, this small stone building was the headquarters of the Democratic Party during the territorial period. Originally, the stone headquarters building was attached to a log cabin. Long since gone, it likely served as the residence of William Simmons and his son, Thomas. The Simmonses had traveled to Kansas Territory from Indiana in 1853, squatting on the land for an entire year before the territory legally opened for settlement.

The family made their living along the Kaw River, where they fished and operated a twenty-foot ferry known as the *Fairy Queen* made from hollowed-out sycamore logs. Their stone building would eventually change from a site of politics to one of commerce. It was acquired by the Atchison, Topeka & Santa Fe Railroad, which utilized the building as a pay station for years. The property was purchased in 1997 by the Istas family, who began reclamation of the site and its grounds. The following year, the Lecompton Historical Society purchased the site, fully restoring it as part of the Historic Lecompton View Park.

COAL CREEK LIBRARY

698 East 1719 Road—Vinland

Located just twelve miles southeast of Lawrence is a small one-story, one-room red brick building with a small porch. This is believed to be the oldest continuously operating library in Kansas. The Coal Creek Library Association was founded in 1859 and has served the community ever since. Neighbors sent ten dollars to Philadelphia to purchase books to establish the library. For the next forty-one years, the library collection was housed in various local homes. In 1900, this library building was constructed on a lot purchased for only ten dollars. It remains open to the public but is only open on Sunday afternoons from April through October. Call ahead to make sure you can visit.

OLD CASTLE MUSEUM

513 5th Street—Baldwin City

Much like the University of Kansas started with one simple building, Baker University started similarly. Known originally as the "College Building," this three-story limestone building was constructed in 1858, becoming Kansas's first four-year university building. Known now as the "Old Castle Building," it currently houses a museum. On display you will find artifacts from the Methodist circuit riders, Santa Fe Trail history, the territorial settlement period and Baker University's history, to which then Senator Abraham Lincoln donated money. The site also includes the Old Palmyra Post Office, Palmyra being the original name of Baldwin City, which once served the travelers passing along the nearby Santa Fe Trail.

Seen in 1958, Old Castle Hall was Baker University's first building and, at the time of construction, the only college building in the state. Today, it houses artifacts from Kansas, Methodist and Baker history. *Courtesy of the Library of Congress.*

OREGON-CALIFORNIA TRAIL SEGMENT AND NATURE TRAIL

867 U.S. Highway 40—Wellsville

Numerous sites abound throughout the area that are related to the overland trails to the West. One such preserved location of wagon rut evidence to this is located near the First United Methodist Church along U.S. Highway 40, just west of Lawrence. From 1840 to 1860, more than 400,000 pioneers traveled along the Oregon and California Trails, most of them passing along this segment of the trails. The route stretched two thousand miles to the Willamette Valley in Oregon or the gold fields in California. Decades of wagon wheels carved ruts into the earth, leaving their imprints in the stone and dirt along the prairies, hills, mountains and rivers. Here, one can view the remnants of such travel and take a hike along the nearby nature trail.

BLACK JACK BATTLEFIELD

163 East 2000 Road—Wellsville

In the predawn hours of June 2, 1856, abolitionist John Brown led his Free State forces into battle against Henry Clay Pate's proslavery militiamen, who were encamped along the Santa Fe Trail. Pate, a twenty-four-year-old Virginian, and his militia were out to get Old Man Brown, as a response to the Pottawatomie Massacre on the night of May 24–25, when Brown and his men hacked to death two men they suspected to be proslavery supporters. Roughly one hundred men fought each other in a three-hour battle that ultimately ended in Brown's favor, with Pate surrendering to the antislavery leader.

In the park surrounding the battlefield, one can find wagon ruts from the Santa Fe Trail, located within the Ivan Boyd Prairie. Near the battlefield is the home of Robert Hall Pearson. Pearson was active in the Free State Party, taking part in the Battles of Franklin and Black Jack and the defense of Lawrence during the Bleeding Kansas period and the pursuits of William Quantrill and General Sterling Price following the Battle of Westport during the Civil War. Afterward, he settled down on his

The Robert Hall Pearson home sits in the Black Jack Battlefield Park, serving as a historic site and headquarters for the interpretation of the historic 1856 battle. *Author's collection.*

homestead, building this home in the 1880s. The house and surrounding land stayed within the Pearson family until 2003. The homestead was purchased by the Friends of Black Jack Battlefield and the Lawrence Preservation Alliance to avert development.

SIGNAL OAK

445 East 1750 Road—Baldwin City

Located atop Santa Fe Ridge and overlooking the Vinland Valley, Signal Oak is located two miles north of Baldwin City. The site played a crucial role during Bleeding Kansas and during the Civil War. Nearby settlers would climb the oak's branches, hanging lanterns at night and flags during the day, signaling other settlers at Blue Mound as an alert; they would then alert those in Lawrence in turn. The signals were warnings from the various communities that invaders were approaching. Although the oak tree died in 1914, a marker and plaque recount its history. On a clear day, you can still get a great view of Blue Mound and Lawrence in the distance.

BIBLIOGRAPHY

BOOKS

Adams, Virginia, Katie Armitage, Donna Butler and Carol Shankel. *On the Hill: A Photographic History of the University of Kansas*. University of Kansas Press, 2007.

Armitage, Katie H. *Lawrence: Survivors of Quantrill's Raid*. Arcadia Publishing, 2010.

Bader, Robert Smith. *Hayseeds, Moralizers, and Methodists: The Twentieth-Century Image of Kansas*. University of Kansas Press, 1988.

———. *Prohibition in Kansas*. University of Kansas Press, 1986.

Bisel, Debra Goodrich, and Richard B. Myers. *The Civil War in Kansas: Ten Years of Turmoil*. Arcadia Publishing, 2017.

Burchill, Mary Dresser, and Norma Decker Hoagland. *The Life and Legacy of Elizabeth Miller Watkins: A Pioneering Philanthropist*. University of Kansas Press, 2023.

Castel, Albert E. *Civil War Kansas: Reaping the Whirlwind*. University of Kansas Press, 1997.

———. *William Clarke Quantrill: His Life and Times*. Oklahoma Press, 1999.

Collins, Joseph T., and Suzanne L. Collins. *Kansas Wetlands: A Wildlife Treasury*. University of Kansas Press, 1994.

Cordley, Richard. *A History of Lawrence, Kansas, From First Settlement to the Close of the Rebellion*. Lawrence Journal Press, 1895.

————. *The Lawrence Massacre by a Band of Missouri Ruffians Under Quantrell.* J.S. Broughton, 1865.

————. *Pioneer Days in Kansas.* Pilgrim Press, 1903.

Dary, David. *More True Tales of Old-Time Kansas.* University of Kansas Press, 1987.

————. *The Santa Fe Trail: Its History, Legends, and Lore.* University of Kansas Press, 2012.

————. *True Tales of Old-Time Kansas.* University of Kansas Press, 1984.

Dean, Virgil W. *Lawrence.* Images of America series. Arcadia Publishing, 2015.

Dean, Virgil W., ed. *John Brown to Bob Dole: Movers and Shakers in Kansas History.* University of Kansas Press, 2006.

Domer, Dennis, and Barbara Watkins, eds. *Embattled Lawrence: Conflict & Community.* University of Kansas Continuing Education, 2001.

Domer, Dennis, ed. *Embattled Lawrence, Kansas: The Enduring Struggle for Freedom.* Douglas County Historical Society & Watkins Community Museum, 2022.

Earle, Jonathan, and Diane Mutti Burke, eds. *Bleeding Kansas, Bleeding Missouri: The Long Civil War on the Border.* University of Kansas Press, 2013.

Etcheson, Nicole. *Bleeding Kansas: Contested Liberty in the Civil War Era.* University of Kansas Press, 2004.

Fitzgerald, Daniel C. *Faded Dreams: More Ghost Towns of Kansas.* University of Kansas Press, 1994.

————. *Ghost Towns of Kansas: A Traveler's Guide.* University of Kansas Press, 1988.

Goodrich, Thomas. *Bloody Bill Anderson: The Short, Savage Life of a Civil War Guerrilla.* Stackpole Books, 1998.

————. *Bloody Dawn: The Story of the Lawrence Massacre.* Kent State University Press, 1991.

Griffin, Clifford S. *The University of Kansas: A History.* University of Kansas Press, 1974.

Heitz, Lisa Hefner. *Haunted Kansas: Ghost Stories and Other Eerie Tales.* University of Kansas Press, 1997.

Hoagland, Norma Decker. *Watkins and Miller Halls: University of Kansas.* University of Kansas Press, 2016.

Hoard, Robert J., and William E. Banks. *Kansas Archaeology.* University of Kansas Press, 2016.

Horowitz, Tony. *Midnight Rising: John Brown and the Raid that Sparked the Civil War.* Picador, 2012.

Jost, Lora, and Dave Lowenstein. *Kansas Murals: A Traveler's Guide*. University of Kansas Press, 2006.

Koch, William E. *Folklore from Kansas: Customs, Beliefs, and Superstitions*. University of Kansas Press, 1980.

Laird, Betty, and Martha Parker. *Soils of Our Souls*. Freedom Publishing Company, 1976.

Larsen, Lawrence H., and Nancy J. Hulston. *The University of Kansas Medical Center: A Pictorial History*. University of Kansas Press, 1992.

Leslie, Edward E. *The Devil Knows How to Ride: The True Story of William Clark Quantrill and His Confederate Raiders*. Random House, 1996.

Miner, Craig. *Kansas: The History of the Sunflower State, 1854–2000*. University of Kansas Press, 2002.

———. *Seeding Civil War: Kansas in the National News, 1854–1858*. University of Kansas Press, 2008.

Miner, Craig, and William E. Unrau. *The End of Indian Kansas: A Study in Cultural Revolution, 1854–1871*. University Press of Kansas, 1977.

Monhollon, Rusty. *This Is America?: The Sixties in Lawrence, Kansas*. Palgrave, 2002.

Morgan, Bill. *Beat Atlas: A State by State Guide to the Beat Generation in America*. City Lights Publishing, 2011.

Pollard, William C., Jr. *Dark Friday: The Story of Quantrill's Raid*. Baranski Publishing Company, 1983.

Potter, David M. *The Impending Crisis, 1848–1861*. Harper Perennial, 2011.

Prescott, Cynthia Culver. *Pioneer Mother Monuments: Constructing Cultural Memory*. University of Oklahoma Press, 2019.

Reynolds, David S. *John Brown, Abolitionist: The Man Who Killed Slavery, Sparked the Civil War, and Seeded Civil Rights*. Vintage Books, 2006.

Rose-Mockry, Katherine. *Liberating Lawrence: Gay Activism in the 1970s at the University of Kansas*. University of Kansas Press, 2024.

Rury, John L., and Kim Cary Warren. *Transforming the University of Kansas: A History, 1965–2015*. University of Kansas Press, 2015.

Sachs, David, and George Erlich. *Guide to Kansas Architecture*. University of Kansas Press, 1996.

Schott, Cindy, and Kathy Schott Gates. *Boys, Let Me Down Easy*. Allen Press, 2005.

Scott, Emory Frank. *One Hundred Years of Lawrence Theatres*. House of Usher, 1979.

Shankel, Carol, and Barbara Watkins. *Old Fraser: The University of Kansas*. Historic Mount Oread Fund, 1984.

Shankel, Carol, and Barbara Watkins, eds. *Spooner Hall: University of Kansas*. Historic Mount Oread Fund, 2009.

Shankel, Carol, Barbara Watkins and Shala Stevenson, eds. *Dyche Hall: University of Kansas Natural History Museum, 1903–2003*. Historic Mount Oread Fund, 2003.

Sullivan, Peggy, and Bill Sharp. *The Dashing Kansan: Lewis Lindsy Dyche: The Amazing Adventures of a Nineteenth-Century Naturalist and Explorer*. Harrow Books, 1990.

Sutton, Robert K. *Stark Mad Abolitionists: Lawrence, Kansas, and the Battle over Slavery in the Civil War Era*. Skyhorse, 2017.

Svobida, Lawrence. *Farming the Dust Bowl: A First-Hand Account from Kansas*. University of Kansas Press, 1986.

Taft, Robert. *The Years at Mt. Oread*. University of Kansas Press, 1955.

Thomas, Paul A. *Haunted Lawrence*. The History Press, 2017.

Travis, Michael. *Celebrating Kansas Breweries: People, Places & Stories*. The History Press, 2022.

Vuckovic, Myriam. *Voices from Haskell: Indian Students Between Two Worlds, 1884–1928*. University of Kansas Press, 2008.

Warner, Chuck. *Birds, Bones, and Beetles: The Improbable Career and Remarkable Legacy of University of Kansas Naturalist Charles D. Bunker*. University of Kansas Press, 2019.

Watson, Blake Andrew. *Kansas and Kansans in World War I: Service at Home and Abroad*. University of Kansas Press, 2024.

White, Richard. *Railroaded: The Transcontinentals and the Making of Modern America*. W.W. Norton, 2011.

White, William Allen. *The Autobiography of William Allen White*. University of Kansas Press, 1990.

Wiechert, Sandra Swanson. *Historic Mount Oread: A Catalog of KU's Landmarks*. Historic Mount Oread Fund. University of Kansas, 1999.

Workers of the Writer's Program of the Works Projects Administration in the State of Kansas. *The WPA Guide to 1930s Kansas*. University of Kansas Press, 1984.

PUBLICATIONS

Adams, Molly. "Return of the Rock Event Coming Up; City of Lawrence Asks Public to Respect Privacy of Other Events." *Lawrence Times*, August 17, 2023.

Armitage, Katie H. "Out of the Ashes: The Rebuilding of Lawrence and the Quest for Quantrill's Raid Claims." *Kansas History: A Journal of the Central Plains* 37 (Winter 2014–15): 226–41.

Belt, Mike. "This Old House: Historic Home Being Restored Inside and Out." *Lawrence Journal-World*, April 22, 2007.

Benson, Sarah. "La Yarda, a Piece of City's Hispanic History." *Lawrence Journal-World*, June 22, 2006.

Black, Brian. "Mastering the Kaw: The Bowersock Dam and the Development of Lawrence Industry." *Kansas History* (1993): 262–275.

Dailey, Dennis M. "Josiah Miller, an Antislavery Southerner: Letters to Father and Mother." *Kansas History* 36, no. 2 (2013).

Goudsouzian, Aram. "'Can Basketball Survive Chamberlain?': The Kansas Years of Wilt the Stilt." *Kansas History: A Journal of the Central Plains* 28, no. 3 (Autumn 2005).

Harper, Tom. "Smith Hall Is an Architectural and Artistic Landmark Worth Saving." *Lawrence Times*, November 2, 2022. https://lawrencekstimes.com/2022/11/02/harper-smith-hall-oped.

Hlavacek, Joanna. "Haskell's Historic, Long-Shuttered Hiawatha Hall Receives New Red Roof; Reopening Still Years Away." *Lawrence Journal-World*, September 14, 2017.

Hodison, Maya "Upcoming Historic Tours of La Yarda to Highlight 'Incredible Story' of the Lawrence Neighborhood." *Lawrence Times*, May 27, 2022.

Kendall, Dave. "A Boulder's Journey: Lawrence Monolith Will Be Returned to the Kaw in Thoughtful Process." *Kansas Reflector*, May 1, 2022.

Lawhorn, Chad. "Famous Criminal Clyde Barrow May Have Gotten Start Robbing Banks in Lawrence." *Lawrence Journal-World*, September 19, 2011.

———. "Historic Castle Tea Room Building to Be Put Up for Lease as Nonprofit Ownership Falls on Hard Times." *Lawrence Journal-World*, April 17, 2019.

———. "Lawhorn's Lawrence: The City's Oldest Home." *Lawrence Journal-World*, December 1, 2023.

———. "Lawrence Convention and Visitors Bureau Plans to Change Name to Explore Lawrence." *Lawrence Journal-World*, April 22, 2015.

Lawrence Daily Journal-World. "Funeral of J.D. Bowersock Held This Afternoon." October 28, 1922, 1.

Michaelis, Patricia. "Quantrill's Raid in Kansas Memory." *Kansas History* 36, no. 3 (September 2013): 198–209.

Nelson, Evert. "Kansas Football Fans Bring Goal Post to Potter Lake after Beating Oklahoma State." *Topeka Capital-Journal*, November 5, 2022.

Paige, DeAsia. "Lawrence-Based Quilter Inspires a New Generation of Artists." *University Daily Kansan*, February 1, 2019.

Roe, Sasha. "Chi Omega Fountain Central to Many KU Traditions." *Lawrence Journal-World*, August 18, 2009.

Rombeck, Terry. "Finishing Touches Put on Korean War Statue." *Lawrence Journal-World*, November 28, 2004.

Spacek, Nick. "Brad Norman Ttalks About His Doc, *The Outhouse The Film*, Which Plays Liberty Hall Saturday." *The Pitch*, October 13, 2017.

Strong, Frank. "The Alumni in the War." *Graduate Magazine of the University of Kansas* (June 1, 1918): 277–91.

Weir, Grayson. "Epic Scenes Unfold as Kansas Students Throw Goalpost in the Lake to Celebrate Bowl Eligibility." *OutKick*, November 6, 2022.

ELECTRONIC SOURCES

Arnold, Jordan, Grant Heiman and Hannah Saxton. "746 Massachusetts Street." Explore Lawrence, January 1, 2017. Retrieved October 19, 2021. https://www.explorelawrence.com/things-to-do/history-heritage/block-by-block/700-block/746-massachusetts-street.

Beaudoin, Jedd. "'The Outhouse' Recaptures Glory of Legendary Lawrence-Area Dive Venue." KMUW, April 12, 2018. Retrieved May 7, 2020. https://www.kmuw.org/post/outhouse-recaptures-glory-legendary-lawrence-area-dive-venue.

Bowersock Power Company. "Our History." Retrieved October 11, 2023. bowersockpower.com.

Free State Brewing Company. "Our Story." January 1, 2017. Retrieved June 26, 2024. http://www.freestatebrewing.com/the-story-of-the-Free-State-Brewing-Co.

Freedom's Frontier National Heritage Area. "Marla Quilts—African American Museum & Textile Academy, Partner Spotlight." January 1, 2016. Retrieved June 8, 2024. https://myemail.constantcontact.com/Partner-Spotlight---Marla-Quilts.html?soid=1102073656590&aid=4vcx0R6B4_8.

Gintowt, Richard. "Inside The Outhouse." February 19, 2003. Retrieved April 2, 2024. http://www.lawrence.com/news/2003/feb/19/inside_the.

Huff, Meredith. "Seedy Business: History of the Barteldes Seed Company." University of Kansas Kenneth Spencer Research Library, February 26, 2019. Retrieved March 15, 2024. https://blogs.lib.ku.edu/spencer/seedy-business-history-of-the-barteldes-seed-company.

Jackson, Marla A. African-American Quilt Museum & Textile Academy, Freedom's Frontier National Heritage Area, January 1, 2020. Retrieved June 2, 2024. http://www.freedomsfrontier.org/Visitors/Sites/Comments.aspx?id=170.

Lawrence Modern. "Beal House (2011)." Retrieved April 3, 2024. https://lawrencemodern.com/bakers-dozen/university-place.

———. "Chewning House (2014)." Retrieved January 5, 2024. https://lawrencemodern.com/bakers-dozen/chewning-house.

Liberty Hall. "History of Liberty Hall." June 1, 2020. Retrieved June 25, 2024. http://libertyhall.net/about/history.

Pincock, Charissa. "Spencer's November-December Exhibit: 'Creating Over a Century of Symphonies: The Reuter Organ Company.'" Kansas University Kenneth Spencer Research Library, Inside Spencer, November 14, 2023. Retrieved November 14, 2023. https://blogs.lib.ku.edu/spencer/spencers-november-december-exhibit-creating-over-a-century-of-symphonies-the-reuter-organ-company.

Potts, Mark. "900 Mississippi Street." November 22, 2019. Lawrence Preservation Alliance. Retrieved March 18, 2024. https://lawrencepreservation.org/award-winners/2019/11/22/900-mississippi-street.

Reuter Organ Company. "Company History (2024)." Retrieved January 19, 2024. https://www.reuterorgan.com/about.

Sacred Red Rock Project. "Background of Inzhujewaxobe." Retrieved September 15, 2023. https://sacredredrock.com/background-of-inzhujewaxobe.

Sunflower Outdoor and Bike. "Celebrating 50 Years of Sunflower Outdoor & Bike." 2023. Retrieved January 24, 2024. sunfloweroutdoorandbike.com.

Unmistakably Lawrence. "921 Massachusetts Street." Retrieved December 9, 2021. https://www.explorelawrence.com/things-to-do/history-heritage/block-by-block/900-block/921-massachusetts-street.

Valverde, Rochelle. "New Project Takes on the Shunganunga Boulder." *Between the Rock and a Hard Place*, January 26, 2020. Retrieved September 15, 2023. https://www.robinsonpark1929.com/news/new-project-takes-on-the-shunganunga-boulder.

OTHER PRINT SOURCES

I utilized the City of Lawrence's Historic Resources Commission resources for its Historic Preservation Landmarks, as well as the Department of the Interior's resources via the National Archives for locations listed in the National Register of Historic Places. These documents provide information on the past and present history of historic locations throughout the region via applications filed with these departments for inclusion on said lists. A listing of every document utilized can be found at the following:

City of Lawrence Historic Resources Commission. Landmark Designation Reports. https://lawrenceks.org/pds/historic_resources.

U.S. Department of the Interior. National Register of Historic Places Nomination Forms—City: Lawrence, KS. https://catalog.archives.gov/search?q=*:*&f.parentNaId=20812721&f.level=fileUnit&sort=titleSort%20asc.

ABOUT THE AUTHOR

Tristan Smith is an independent historian living in Houston, Texas. He has worked for museums and nonprofits in Kansas, Missouri and Texas for more than twenty years in marketing, curatorial, education, volunteer, management and administrative capacities. Museums he's been involved with have featured natural history, the 1950s, fine art, community history, a sunken steamboat found in a Kansas corn field, a U.S. president and fire history. He has also consulted for organizations and municipalities in historic preservation. He is the author of *Houston Fire Department* (Images of America, Arcadia Publishing, 2015), *A History Lover's Guide to Houston* (The History Press, 2020), *Historic Cemeteries of Houston and Galveston* (The History Press, 2023), *A History Lover's Guide to Galveston* (The History Press, 2024) and the forthcoming *Treasures of Texas: National Historic Landmarks of the Lone Star State* (Schiffer Publishing, 2025).